See You at the Pole and other prayer movements are strong evidence that young people can be at the forefront of a spiritual awakening in our generation—especially if they are given practical guidance and the opportunity to pray. In *Youth Ministry on Your Knees*, Mike Higgs offers the kind of vision and practicality that we need for today. I can't think of a better person than Mike to write this book, and I hope every youth worker will read and learn from it!

—Doug Clark, promotion coordinator, See You at the Pole,
director of field ministries, National Network of Youth Ministries

"Don't turn here for gimmicks to hype and dazzle people into short-lived prayer binges. Mike Higgs offers seasoned wisdom to lead people to pray with persistent passion. His style of writing matches the authenticity and honesty of his years of walking with young people. You're going to have fun reading this book. If you live it with others, you'll be praying your way with others into the grand purposes of God—and that's what we're all hungry for.'

—Steve Hawthorne, director, WayMakers

"I see only two possible futures for this generation of students. They may become the next revival generation, leading the church into full revival and then culture into full transformation. Or they may witness the final crumbling of culture and the resulting chaos and judgment that will go with it. Either way, there will be a desperate need for them to live on their knees, and that never will happen until the key adults in their lives start living on their knees as well. I know the heart of Mike Higgs. His humility, his faithfulness in the ministry of prayer and his clear thinking on building prayer strategies make him just the one to write this book. He has given an important gift to student ministry."

—Richard Ross, Ph.D., spokesperson, True Love Waits

"Always recognizing that the greatest need in the believing youth of today is spiritual Fatherhood and mentoring, Mike Higgs shares out of the integrity, honesty, and transparency, which have become his trademarks. Presenting illustrations drawn from experience, Mike powerfully demonstrates that the best teaching is accomplished by honest example. He also explores the bottom line that all effective prayer begins and ends with maintaining a pure heart and a heart posture of wanting to please the Father. Although written primarily for youth workers, this book will revive and refurbish the heart of every leader and believer who reads it."

—Gary P. Bergel, president, Intercessors for America/Youth Interceding for America

"Mike Higgs' new book hits the nail right on the head! Most of us who are youth ministry veterans of twenty years or more have come to the same conclusion, both by experience and the Spirit's leading. But Mike, in his own special style that makes you chuckle at the honest exposure of his journey and then weep as the truth of the relevance of it hits home in yours, has had the guts to put it on paper! I say guts for two reasons: first, because it needed to be said, and second, because it had to come from someone who actually lives it. We at the Metro City Leaders of the National Network of Youth Ministries have always asked Mike to lead us as our Hero into the Throne room of our Lord and King because he knows the way by heart!"

—Mark Whittaker, director, Youth Outreach Network

YOUTH MINISTRY ON YOUR KNEES:
MENTORING AND MOTIVATING YOUTH TO PRAY

By Mike Higgs

NAVPRESS®

BRINGING TRUTH TO LIFE

OUR GUARANTEE TO YOU

We believe so strongly in the message of our books that we are making this quality guarantee to you. If for any reason you are disappointed with the content of this book, return the title page to us with your name and address and we will refund to you the list price of the book. To help us serve you better, please briefly describe why you were disappointed. Mail your refund request to: NavPress, P.O. Box 35002, Colorado Springs, CO 80935.

Pray! Books are published by NavPress. NavPress is the publishing ministry of The Navigators, an international Christian organization whose mission is to reach, disciple, and equip people to know Christ and to make Him known through successive generations.

ISBN 1-57683-618-5

Chapter 6 of this book is adapted from *Youth Ministry from the Inside Out* by Mike Higgs. Copyright © 2003 by Mike Higgs. Used by permission of InterVarsity Press, P. O. Box 1400, Downers Grove, IL 60515, USA.

Library of Congress Cataloging-in-Publication Data

Higgs, Mike, 1954-
   Youth ministry on your knees : mentoring and mobilizing young people
to pray / by Mike Higgs.—1st ed.
      p. cm.
   Includes bibliographical references.
   ISBN 1-57683-618-5
1. Church work with youth.   2. Prayer—Christianity. 3.
Youth—Religious life.   I. Title.
   BV4447.H485 2004
   259'.23—dc22

                                        2004025904

Printed in Canada
1 2 3 4 5 6 7 8 9 10 / 09 08 07 06 05

Visit the *Pray!* website at www.praymag.com
Contact the author at mikehiggs@integrity.com

CONTENTS

To my children, Lillian and Levi,
whose simple yet powerful prayers of faith
warm the hearts of their earthly daddy and their heavenly Father.

ACKNOWLEDGMENTS

"It takes a village to grow a child." Or something like that. I do know that it takes a "village" of help to grow a book! And my village is legion. Thanks to Jon Graf for recruiting me to take on this project, to Dave Wilson and Joyce Dinkins for helping me fine-tune my original writing, and to *Pray!* Books and the NavPress folks for taking a chance by publishing a prayer book that targets the "niche" market of youth ministry.

Thanks to my long-distance mentors, David Bryant and Gary Bergel, for your invaluable support and encouragement as I have stumbled along in this mushrooming prayer movement. You have no idea how profoundly you have marked me. Thanks to my local mentor, Joe Aldrich, who blazed the trail for much of what I do and has taught me, among many other things, the vital role united prayer plays in building a youth ministry movement that has an impact on the city.

Thanks to the late Terry Dirks for helping me gain perspective as I have sought to "think globally and act locally" in the arena of prayer. Thanks to the Portland Youth Foundation Ministry Council members for our twelve-year partnership in putting these ideas into action on a grassroots level. Thanks to Youth for Christ's DC/LA Ministries, Young Life Pacific Northwest, the National Network of Youth Ministries, and the other groups who have let me "practice" prayer mobilization and support at their events.

Thanks to my bride and soul mate, Terri, a woman of prayer who models for me the surrendered life that makes prayer without ceasing possible. And thank You, Jesus, through whose name we can have the access, intimacy, and continual communion we were created to enjoy with the Father!

FOREWORD

The LORD says to my Lord: "Sit at my right hand until I make your enemies a footstool for your feet." The LORD will extend your mighty scepter from Zion; you will rule in the midst of your enemies. Your troops will be willing on your day of battle. Arrayed in holy majesty, from the womb of the dawn [just after the darkest hour, in the beauty of holiness—intercessory worship garments] you will receive the dew of your youth.

—Psalm 110:1-3

Some understand this passage (which I have commented on in brackets) as a prophetic picture describing the global arising of a last-days youth army of prayer. Out of the darkest hour I have personally seen them appearing.

On September 2, 2000, the morning of The Call DC, I awoke early. At the first light of dawn I saw them "glistening like dew." By 6:30 A.M., an estimated two hundred thousand young people had already gathered on that battlefield of prayer. And over the day some four hundred thousand wept and worshiped, prayed and prophesied and, we believe, altered history. From See You at the Pole to The Call, the youth prayer movement has arrived!

Millions of Muslims fast thirty days a year at Ramadan and pray five times a day. Theirs is a culture of prayer, while the church simply dabbles in it. God wants a house of prayer that will contend with every other house. Youth sense this, and everywhere they are beginning to fast and pray. They are bored with religion; they want the real deal. They want God and they are returning to the only place they can find Him—the house of prayer and worship. Every day I see them: twenty-one day fasts, all-night prayer meetings, See You at the Pole. Before it's over, revivals will be birthed in schools, stadiums will be filled, and governments will be shaken.

When Jesus left earth, the only visible evidence that He had been here was a prayer meeting comprised of 120 desperate followers. I thank God for the new breed of leaders redirecting our youth back to this root—men like Tom Sipling of 30 Second Kneel Down, Richard Mull with the 40-Day Revolution of Fasting, Mike Bickle of the twenty-four hour International Houses of Prayer, and Pete Greig with the global 24/7 prayer movement. Mike Higgs—a true father to the youth prayer movement—is a "no-namer" before men but a man known at God's throne. With refreshing clarity, my friend Mike describes the present-day youth prayer movement and gives clear vision to where we are going and how to get there.

Twenty years ago I was employed in youth ministry. During that time, my youth group dwindled from seventy to one. Literally, I ended up with one. I tried so hard to make the machinery go and grow, but failed. After I was released from my position I started a small prayer meeting. That's where the power is! The Spirit of God came down and a little Jesus movement sprang up supernaturally. I wish I could have read this book as a youth minister. It may have spared me years of pain and problems.

As I look on the futuristic landscape of America, I see clouds of darkness and dread looming—the collapse of law, the decline of morality, and antichrist agendas mounting. I could be tempted to acquiesce to a counsel of despair. But when I hear seasoned youth leaders who have become spiritual fathers—men like Mike Higgs—emerging to call youth ministers and ministries out of burnt-out, entertainment-based ministry into the passion-fueled furnace of prayer and intimacy, hope arises in me. I believe we will experience a revolution of righteousness and harvest in the nation as a result.

We've been teaching our children to fast and pray. The times *demand* that they fast and pray! Get the bread of this book in your belly—then go mobilize these sons and daughters for a new American Revolution!

Lou Engle, Pasadena, California
June 2004

INTRODUCTION:
LOOK OUT, WORLD! HELP FOR THE STRUGGLE

Somebody once said, "Context is everything." While I don't adhere to that mindset completely, it certainly holds true in regard to the theme of this book. An author hopes his book will have a long "shelf life." So when he writes he usually avoids too many references to contemporary context—by the time a reader picks up the book, the context may have changed significantly! However, in this case some context is helpful.

I am putting the finishing touches on this book in the context of significant upheaval on a number of fronts. My country has been immersed in a war in the Middle East that has been a struggle at best, and the strategy for bringing peace and stability to that part of the world is being questioned by many. Soldiers and civilians are dying daily. Struggle has become fodder for an increasingly contentious political battle during an election year. Culture wars on the home front have escalated. I have the dubious distinction of living in the state of Oregon, where both assisted suicide and same-sex marriages are taking place. Over the airwaves, right-wing and left-wing pundits lob verbal grenades back and forth with increasing vitriol. Popular reality TV shows demean people and promote unethical and immoral behavior. In pondering all of this, I can't help but be drawn to the numerous biblical examples of those who cried out to God in the face of calamity.

David called upon God in the face of national famine, war against the Philistines, and attacks from Saul. David sang praises to God:

I will call on the LORD, who is worthy of praise, for he saves me from my enemies. . . . In my distress I cried out to the LORD; yes, I called to my God for help. He heard me from his sanctuary; my cry reached his ears. . . . He reached down from heaven and rescued me. . . . As for God, his way is perfect. All the LORD's promises prove true. He is a shield for all who look to him for protection.

—2 Samuel 22:4,7,17,31, NLT

Then there's the testimony of the Israelite armies, tribes east of the Jordan who waged war against their enemies, the Hagrites and their alliance:

There were 44,760 skilled warriors in the armies of Reuben, Gad, and the half-tribe of Manasseh. They cried out to God during the battle, and he answered their prayer because they trusted in him. So the Hagrites and all their allies were defeated.

—1 Chronicles 5:18,20, NLT

What about the story of King Jehoshaphat and the nation of Judah?[1] During a period of relative peace, King 'Phat (his street name) was informed that big-time trouble was on the way:

After this, the Moabites and Ammonites with some of the Meunites came to make war on Jehoshaphat. Some men came and told Jehoshaphat, "A vast army is coming against you from Edom, from the other side of the Sea. It is already in Hazazon Tamar" (that is, En Gedi).

—2 Chronicles 20:1-2

Apparently, the size of the approaching army, with all the "-ites," was unusually large; and for some reason they were already much too close for Jehoshaphat and Judah to respond as they normally would when facing an impending battle. So Jehoshaphat responded with a call for national prayer and fasting, to inquire of the Lord as to what to do to avoid calamity and defeat. His passionate prayer in the assembly of Judah ended thusly:

> "For we have no power to face this vast army that is attacking us. *We do not know what to do, but our eyes are upon you.*"
>
> —2 Chronicles 20:12 (emphasis added)

Similarly, when Nehemiah heard the terrible news of Jerusalem's devastation, he fasted and prayed:

> O Lord, God of heaven, the great and awesome God who keeps his covenant of unfailing love with those who love him and obey his commands, listen to my prayer! Look down and see me praying night and day for your people Israel.
>
> —Nehemiah 1:5-6, NLT

Meanwhile, in Persia, Queen Esther appealed to God to save the Jews from massacre during the reign of King Xerxes. Haman, an evil advisor to the king, plotted against the Jews, but Esther prayed:

> Go and gather all the Jews of Susa and fast for me. Do not eat or drink for three days, night or day. My maids and I will do the same.
>
> —Esther 4:16, 8:7,8, NLT

When calamity is in our context—be it military war, culture war, or the ongoing war for the lives of the kids we love and minister among—we are called to use today the same weapon these biblical people successfully used against overwhelming odds and insurmountable obstacles: prayer. For all of these "wars" are battles and skirmishes in the all-encompassing kingdom war that has ensued throughout human history.

By the time you read this, the context may have changed significantly, and you may not sense the same urgency that I do as I write. But don't be deceived; the war rages on. Ultimately we must admit that when it comes to contending for the souls of kids, despite cutting-edge youth ministry philosophies, programs, and strategies, we don't know what to do either—except pray.

Before you jump deeper into this book, let me set the stage for what follows. Because many of us are youth workers, it's appropriate to provide an anecdote:

> A motorist was unknowingly caught in an automated speed trap that measured his speed using radar and photographed his car. He later received in the mail a ticket for forty dollars and a photo of his car. Instead of payment, he sent the police department a photograph of forty dollars. Several days later, he received a letter from the police that contained another picture, this time of handcuffs. He immediately mailed in his forty dollars.

For those of us in youth ministry, prayer is something we often talk about, read about, teach our kids about, and feel guilty about. We take plenty of "photos" of prayer. While these are all worthwhile endeavors (except perhaps the guilt), isn't the essence of prayer the "hard currency" of *doing* it? In the pages that follow, you will find plenty of information and even theology concerning prayer (all needed), but you will also find lots of prayer models and examples of prayer in action. The text includes ways to help students pray for their schools and classmates; helps for youth workers seeking to integrate prayer into the fabric of their youth ministries; and models of prayer strategies that can help transform ministries, campuses, and communities. My desire is that these models and ideas will motivate and inspire you to develop your own prayer strategies.

It is critical to use this book as part (and only part) of your own growing "toolbox" of prayer resources. Ask the Holy Spirit to guide you in picking out the ideas or tools that are for you and your ministry—don't try to utilize them all. I will continue to emphasize this idea throughout this book: God gives us our own custom-tailored, need-specific prayer strategies and ideas—if we *ask*, and then *listen* (see Jeremiah 29:1-13).

Full disclosure is also in order here. I have well over 100 books on my shelves that have to do with some aspect of prayer, most written by powerful prayer warriors. Some of these authors lead international prayer ministries; others are widely respected teachers and mentors; many are gifted intercessors. I don't seem to fit in any of those categories as well as I would like. A significant part of my ministry over the past twelve years has been given to facilitating united prayer among youth and youth workers and mobilizing prayer support for youth ministry conferences and events. Sometimes folks assume that because I mobilize prayer, I must be a big-league intercessor. Rees Howell and George Müller were big-league intercessors. I'm just a youth worker trying his best to grow in the area of prayer, and trying in these pages to help my fellow youth workers—and others who love kids—do likewise.

Intercession does not appear to be specifically identified in Scripture as a spiritual gift, although some would argue otherwise.[2] That being said, it is recognized increasingly today that God has wired certain folks to engage in prayer in extraordinary ways. Some of the intercessors I know get up well before the sun, head for their prayer closets, and emerge several hours later with puffy eyes and a smile, having just prayed for most of the inhabited planet. And it came as easy for them as breathing. For me, several hours in a prayer closet could on occasion be called an extended nap. I wish I could say intercession comes as naturally for me as breathing, but the truth is, my praying is often a discipline that must be renewed regularly, if not daily. It is often hard work. My thoughts wander; I get behind on interceding for others; on occasion I still tell someone I will pray for him or her, and then forget to do it.

I don't try to excuse my struggles in prayer as simply not being "gifted" in that area. Mark, a friend from college days, leads the prayer ministry at a large church in my city. He says, "If prayer was a spiritual gift, some people would feel let 'off the hook,' and excuse their prayerlessness as a lack of gifting. We are *all* called to be people of prayer." I couldn't agree more. God calls us all to be faithful in prayer (Romans 12:12). Praying continually (1 Thessalonians 5:17) is not optional, nor is being devoted to prayer (1 Corinthians 7:5; Colossians 4:2). And we are *all* called to be clear minded and self-controlled in our praying (1 Peter 4:7), which is where the discipline comes into play. So, I keep my lofty personal prayer goals and persevere, knowing that even if I don't transform into a closet warrior, my seasons of intimate communion with the Father will increase in quantity and quality.

They will for you as well. If we are honest, we will admit that many of us in youth ministry are not strong pray-ers. If we are *really* honest, we will probably admit that many of us (perhaps most of us?) struggle in the area of prayer. I don't say that to indict youth workers; there are plenty of non-youth workers who fit this description as well! Rather, I say this because I am convinced that if we are going to have the measure of spiritual influence and impact on the emerging generations of youth that we desire (the inference here, obviously, is that we currently are not; I will support that assertion later), we must grow in our understanding and practice of prayer—both individually and corporately. We must become—or at least be on the growth curve toward becoming—men and women of prayer. Our ministries must feature more than a "prayer base." They must become prayer-driven, prayer-infused, and prayer-bathed.

Note that I said we must grow in both our *understanding* and *practice* of prayer. Although I'm including plenty of stories and models, I also realize that sometimes our failure to grow in the area of prayer is not because we need better ideas, but because we need better theology. I'm not a theologian per se, but I will play one in this book in an attempt to help us better understand the biblical underpinnings of various aspects of prayer. Just don't expect me to wow you with my theological profundity.[3] I'll leave that for the human thermometers (folks who have lots of degrees—M.Div., D.Min., Th.D, Ph.D.). But I'll do my best to give you what I think you need to know as concisely as possible.

My primary target audience for this book is youth workers, both vocational and volunteer. I am one of you. My passion for prayer is joined by my passion for youth ministry. I also have in mind parents and others who have a heart for kids. If you fit in one of those latter categories, I trust you will find information in the pages to follow that is helpful. If we all work together to model prayer, mentor kids in prayer, and motivate them to pray—then, look out world!

Notes

1. I go into this passage in depth in my book, *Youth Ministry from the Inside Out.* (Downers Grove, Ill.: InterVarsity, 2003).
2. See C. Peter Wagner, *Your Spiritual Gifts Can Help Your Church Grow* (Ventura, Calif.: Regal Books, 1997).
3. Profundity: "Deep, thorough, or mature understanding; wisdom, insight, sagaciousness, sagacity, sageness, sapience." (American Heritage Dictionary, version 3.0.1 for Macintosh.) You'll soon find out I don't have a whole lot of profundity, but it's a cool word, huh?

PART I: THE PRAYING IMPERATIVE

1. PRAYER IS NOT A "FLAVOR OF THE MONTH"

The Life of Prayer! Great and sacred theme! It leads us into the Holy of Holies and the secret place of the Most High. It is the very life of the Christian, and it touches the life of God Himself.

—A. B. Simpson, founder,
Christian and Missionary Alliance

When I was a brand new, wet-behind-the-ears youth worker, our church began to investigate a new style of youth ministry that was proving to be extremely successful at attracting unchurched kids to hear the gospel message. The ministry style, and the philosophy behind it, was called Son City. You may not have heard of it, but you likely have heard of the little church that grew out of the original Son City in the Chicago suburbs. The last time I heard, Willow Creek Community Church was still attracting a few folks to their services. Son City was catching on in other venues, and soon our intrepid team of novice youth workers traveled about two hours north on a Wednesday night to see a Son City in action.

We were blown away. Hundreds of kids were crammed into the church youth room. The evening featured team competition that engaged almost everyone. Live, quality music and thoughtful, often humorous drama was played out on the stage. Multi-projector slide shows presented the evening's theme in a creative way. The message was tailored to provide biblical answers to typical teen issues—dating and sex, loneliness, peer pressure. It wasn't long before our fledgling ministry was divided into teams, a live band was assembled, and I learned how to run the dissolve unit that controlled multiple slide projectors. It worked! Our ministry grew by leaps and bounds. Yet eight years later, Son City no longer existed at our church, at least in that form. We had moved on to another ministry style, seeking to adjust our methodology to the continually changing youth culture.

Contemporary youth ministry has always been most effective when responding to current trends in the youth culture and adopting such trends in ministry strategy. The huge Youth for Christ rallies that drew thousands of kids in the 1950s eventually gave way to the more intimate Young Life gatherings of the 1960s and '70s that met in students' homes. These in turn gave way to other culturally relevant styles. Those of us who have been in youth ministry long enough to be just a bit cynical sometimes joke about what will be the next "flavor of the month" youth ministry style. Yet this strength of youth ministry—the ability to adjust in order to be culturally relevant—can also be a weakness when it comes to prayer. There is some danger that we will treat the current explosive growth of prayer as a "flavor of the month," rather than putting it in its rightful place as one of the preeminent acts of youth ministry.

All three Synoptic Gospels record Jesus' response to a question from the Pharisees,[1] who were practicing the spiritual discipline of fasting and wondering why His disciples were not doing likewise. In the context of Jesus' reply that there would indeed come a time when His disciples would fast, Luke records a parable told by Jesus that for our purposes is most instructive: "And no one pours new wine into old wineskins. If he does, the new wine will burst the skins, the wine will run out and the wineskins will be ruined. No, new wine must be poured into new wineskins" (Luke 5:37-38).

Whereas contemporary wine aficionados may highly prize a vintage bottle of the fruit of the vine, wine in Jesus' time didn't ferment gracefully or preserve well. In a porous wine-skin, the unchecked fermentation process would eventually produce vinegar, which is why the Old Testament considers "new wine" a blessing,[2] and why Jesus mentions new wine in His parable, rather than Chateau Galilee Vintage 65 B.C.

Jesus does not specifically identify the "new wine." But the inference is clear: New wine is the gospel of Jesus Christ, foreshadowed and prophesied throughout the Old Testament and now revealed as "new" through the incarnation. The wineskins are the means by which this new wine is presented to the world. Howard Snyder comments,

> Jesus distinguishes here between something essential and primary (the wine) and something secondary but also necessary and useful (the wineskins). Wineskins would be superfluous without the wine they were meant to hold. This is vital for the everyday life of the church. There is that which is new and potent and essential—the gospel of Jesus Christ. And there is that which is secondary, subsidiary, man-made. These are the wineskins, and include traditions, structures and patterns of doing things that have grown up around the gospel.[3]

Obviously, spiritual "new wine" is made such by the working of a God who always will make all things new (Revelation 21:5). New wineskins are our continually evolving and adjusting methods of presenting the gospel message in word and deed. Snyder adds, "For the wineskins are the point of contact between the wine and the world. . . . Wineskins result when the divine gospel touches human culture."[4]

Modern youth ministry has become adept at developing culturally relevant and appropriate wineskins for presenting the gospel to young people. Son City, with all the competition, live music, multimedia, and drama was a wildly effective wineskin, as were Youth For Christ Saturday night rallies and the myriad other strategies that have come and gone over the decades. As contemporary youth culture has become more and more splintered, the wineskins have likewise diversified. For instance, now we are seeing edgy "rave" outreaches, meditative gatherings with candles and incense where students "share their stories," and unapologetic worship experiences with an intense vertical focus. Like I said, youth work is one of the better ministries of the church at discerning cultural trends and developing effective, contextualized means of getting the gospel out and making disciples.

At this point you might be wondering how this relates to prayer as a "flavor of the month." Here it is: Prayer has become a bit "trendy" these days, and a clear and present danger for us in youth ministry is that we treat prayer as a trendy wineskin. Remember the more than 100 prayer-focused titles on my bookshelves that I referred to in the introduction to this book? When I started doing youth ministry there may not have been 100 books on prayer in print, period. Today, type "pray" in the search window of Amazon.com and you get 17,063 book titles. *The Prayer of Jabez* alone has sold eight million copies (plus or minus a few million).

The World Prayer Center in Colorado Springs, Colorado, connects millions of praying believers worldwide. When my mom developed complications after open-heart surgery, I sent a request out to my ministry's prayer team.[5] The next day, I received an email from the World Prayer Center telling me that my request had been forwarded to them, and approximately twenty-thousand people were praying for my mom! Prayer has exploded in popularity, not only within the church but also outside the church walls. Many of the current medical studies on the role of prayer in healing have been funded by secular sources. I'm sure the number of people praying during the initial days of Operation Iraqi Freedom far exceeded just believers.

Much of this upsurge in interest is the legitimate response of a discerning church: "He who has an ear, let him hear what the Spirit says to the churches" (Revelation 2:7, see also

2:11,17,29; 3:6,13,22). God is calling His people to pray as never before, and they are responding. There is nothing trendy about the millions of intercessors who mobilized to effectively pray the gospel into the nations within the 10/40 Window, or the prayer leaders from across the country who have met twice annually for more than twenty-five years as America's National Prayer Committee, or the million-plus believers who have committed to intercede on a regular basis as members of the Presidential Prayer Team. A sizeable book could be written that chronicles this modern-day explosion of prayer. But we would be less than honest if we didn't admit that there is a trendy dimension to this prayer movement. A visit to most Christian book and gift stores will make that clear (I'll spare you the specific examples—you know what I mean).

Now, you may be rejoicing as much as I am at this new popularity of prayer, but it is *very* important for us to realize that prayer is *not* a trendy wineskin. Prayer is not primarily culture-bound or culturally relevant, although its expressions may at times be so. And while prayer forms may adjust or shift, the essence of prayer does not. Rather, prayer is our relational connection with the Maker of new spiritual wine. Prayer also is the *primary* means of delivering new wine, through a new wineskin, to an unbelieving world. Also, prayer is our primary method of discovering what wineskins will best serve as the ideal point of contact for the wine and the world. And prayer is much more, as the following pages will demonstrate.

Prayer should be one of the preeminent acts of youth ministry. As wonderful and useful as the various stylistic and programmatic wineskins have been to youth workers seeking to reach kids for Christ, they will continue to evolve, mutate, and adjust with the culture. There will be new youth ministry trends in the years and decades to come. New programs will hit the marketplace. New, effective outreaches will surface. New materials will be published. There will probably even be new games.[6] These will all come and go. But prayer will not leave us.

Prayer is decidedly not a flavor of the month. It has come in a new way, with a new urgency and a renewed passion, in these latter days. It *must* be fully embraced by youth ministry and by youth workers—by you and your ministry—if we are to reach the emerging generations of at-risk youth. We must act *now*.

Notes

1. Matthew, Mark, and Luke are called the Synoptic ("seen together") Gospels because all three chronicle many similar events and teachings, while the Gospel of John is more distinct in content.
2. See also Genesis 27:28; 2 Kings 18:32; Proverbs 3:10; Joel 2:19.
3. Howard A. Snyder, *The Problem of Wineskins: Church Structure in a Technological Age* (Downers Grove, Ill.: InterVarsity, 1975), p. 13.
4. Snyder, pp. 13-14.
5. I will more fully develop the prayer team concept in chapter 7.
6. Two of the better game books that I utilized in my early years of youth work were entitled, appropriately, *The New Games Book* and *More New Games* (Doubleday/Dolphin). And I still use them today with my own two kids!

2. PRAYER PRIMER 101

The purpose of all prayer is to find God's will and to make that will our prayer.
—Catherine Marshall

Prayer is not an argument with God to persuade Him to move things our way, but an exercise by which we are enabled by His Spirit to move ourselves His way.
—Leonard Ravenhill

It is hard to imagine a person intent on growing in prayer who has not pondered questions like these: Why pray? If God is sovereign, why is prayer necessary? Does God always answer prayer? Why is prayer so hard?

I have grappled with these so-called "tough questions" both personally (in my own spiritual journey) and corporately (teaching and training youth and youth workers) long enough to be at least reasonably comfortable with them. That is not to say that I have all the answers, or that devoting a chapter to them titled "Prayer Primer 101" does not make me nervous, because it does. But being nervous is not always a bad thing. I get nervous when my daughter plays solos on her violin, or my son steps into the batter's box against a twelve-year-old flamethrower who only occasionally hits the catcher's mitt. My daughter may hit a rare sour note; my son may occasionally strike out. But in both cases, the reward is worth the risk on their part as well as the nervousness on my part. So, I may hit the occasional sour note, or even strike out a few times when it comes to my so-called "answers" to tough questions regarding prayer, but I'm casting nervousness aside and going for it anyway! With apologies to the movie *Dead Poets Society*: "Carpe diem gloria Deo."[1]

Why pray?

There are myriad legitimate biblical answers to this question, but I want to focus here on one simple answer because I think it sums up all the rest: We pray because we were created to do so. We were created to have an intimate, ongoing personal relationship with the God of the universe in order to walk "in the garden in the cool of the day" (Genesis 3:8) with our Creator. When God said, "Let us make man in our image, in *our* likeness" (Genesis 1:26, note my emphasis on the plural *our*), part of that image and likeness is the capacity for loving relationships, not only horizontally with other men and women of the creation, but also vertically with God. Someone smart[2] once said that we all have a God-shaped hole or void within us that only He can fill.

God, in His sovereignty, has chosen to expand the parameters of trinitarian love and unity to include you and me, creating us so that we might share an interpersonal relationship with Him. This relationship is expressed by and nurtured and developed through communication between the Lover—God—and the beloved—us. And the communication dimension of our developing relationship is prayer. Obviously sin obstructs the prayer dimension of this Lover-beloved relationship: "Surely the arm of the LORD is not too short to save, nor his ear too dull to hear. But your iniquities have separated you from your God; your sins have hidden his face from you, so that he will not hear" (Isaiah 59:1-2).

Yet the story of the Bible, from Adam and Eve's cataclysmic blunder to the death and resurrection of Christ (which was the payment for our sins and allowed us to come into relationship with God), is one of the Lover's initiatives. Sin short-circuited the relationship in the Garden and continues to do so today, but Christ's sacrifice restores the connection. Because of this love, we have the privilege of developing an intimate relationship with our Creator—through prayer.[3]

If God is sovereign, why is prayer necessary?

This question may not be very relevant in the context of the relationship-nurturing dimension of prayer. But when it comes to prayer requests—asking for help, intercession for others, etc.—it's a logical, legitimate question. If God is absolutely, completely in control of all things, and if He is omniscient (all-knowing) and the other "omnis" (omnipotent or all-powerful, and omnipresent or all-present) then why do we need to ask and intercede? Isn't He going to do what He pleases, in accordance with His eternal purposes, regardless of what we may or may not ask in prayer?

I love the fact that the question of prayer's relevance takes us to the intersection of the "expressway" of God's sovereignty and the "freeway" of man's freedom of choice. I love it that our puny, finite minds cannot really configure this intersection despite centuries of dialogue, discussion, debate, and/or dispute. The polar extremes of the issue are well known: if God is totally sovereign, men are robots with no freedom of choice; if men have complete freedom of choice, then God's sovereignty is limited by their choices. There are numerous passages in Scripture that support both sides of this issue. Which, again, is why I love the question originally posed!

If we admit that the reconciliation of these two options (or, the proper configuration of this intersection, if you are still following my previous metaphor) is beyond our human understanding, there are some responses to the question "Why pray?" that I find helpful. Richard Foster offers the first: "The most straightforward answer to this question is simply that God likes to be asked. We like our children to ask us for things that we already know they need because the very asking enhances and deepens the relationship."[4] I like that response because it emphasizes the relational dimension of prayer. Dutch Sheets has a great response as well:

> Here we have, I believe, the reason for the necessity of prayer. God chose, from the time of the Creation, to work on earth through humans, not independent of them. He always has and always will, even at the cost of becoming one. Though God is sovereign and all-powerful, Scripture clearly tells us that He limited Himself, concerning the affairs of the earth, to working through human beings.
>
> Is this not the reason the earth is in such a mess? Not because God wills it so, but because of His need to work and carry out His will through people. . . .
>
> Doesn't He need us to ask for His kingdom to come, His will to be done (see Matthew 6:10)? Surely He wouldn't want us to waste our time asking for something that was going to happen anyway, would He?
>
> Didn't He tell us to ask for our daily bread (see Matthew 6:11)? And yet, He knows our needs before we even ask.
>
> Didn't He tell us to ask that laborers be sent into the harvest (see Matthew 9:38)? But, doesn't the Lord of the harvest want that more than we do?
>
> Didn't Paul say, "Pray for us that the word of the Lord may spread rapidly and be glorified" (2 Thessalonians 3:1)? Wasn't God already planning to do this?
>
> Are not these things God's will? Why, then, am I supposed to ask Him for something He already wants to do if it's not that my asking somehow releases Him to do it?[5]

Catch that last statement by Sheets: *My asking somehow releases Him to do it.* God wants, and in a way we will likely not comprehend while on earth, *needs* our prayers. I realize that some may struggle with that notion (I told you at the start that I was nervous—with good reason!) because it can be read to imply that God is lacking in something we need to supply.

That is *not* the case. God is all-sufficient, but as C. Peter Wagner states, "We must understand that our sovereign God has for His own reasons so designed this world that much of what is truly His will He makes contingent on the attitudes and actions of human beings."[6] Jack Hayford adds, "Prayer is essentially a partnership of the redeemed child of God working hand-in-hand with God toward the realization of His redemptive purposes on earth."[7] Our prayers can release the power and purposes of God—as we pray according to His will.

So, a sovereign God has chosen to allow His eternal purposes to be actualized through the prayers of His people, and He prefers it to be this way. What an amazing privilege we have . . . and what an awesome responsibility as well.

Does God always answer prayer?

Absolutely—at least most of the time. Actually, God always answers our prayers *if* we are praying from a *biblical position*, and *if* we are praying *biblical prayers*. What do I mean by this? Praying from a *biblical position* means praying with what the Bible calls "clean hands and a pure heart" (Psalm 24:4). This is Christianity 101, right? Unconfessed sin = broken relationship with God = unheard prayers:

> If I had cherished sin in my heart, the Lord would not have listened; but God has surely listened and heard my voice in prayer. Praise be to God, who has not rejected my prayer or withheld his love from me!
>
> —Psalm 66:18-20

Likewise, Proverbs 28:13 tells us, "He who conceals his sins does not prosper, but whoever confesses and renounces them finds mercy." If we are in sin, realize it, and subsequently refuse to do anything about it, our prayers have as much chance of reaching heaven as a Tiger Woods' tee shot does of entering an orbit around the earth.

I have found this to be a major reason for the lack of effective prayer, both in my own experience and in the experience of many young people. Usually it's not that we are sinning and don't realize it; as Christians we have a built-in sin alarm known as the Holy Spirit. Rather, we are either immersed in sin and understand that sin blocks our prayers, so we don't even bother to try, or we try to pray through our sin, find it a fruitless endeavor, and eventually abandon it. Or we nurture attitudes that block or hinder our prayers:

- Unforgiveness (Matthew 5:23-24)
- Wrong motives (James 4:3)
- Unbiblical priorities (Colossians 3:2)
- Indifference (Revelation 3:14-17)
- Lack of persistence (Luke 11:5-10; 18:1-8)
- Ignorance, lack of understanding (Job 42:3)

Much of this falls under the heading of "impurity," which we will examine in more detail in the pages to come.

Besides praying from a *biblical position*, we must pray *biblical prayers*, which means praying according to God's will. There are different categories of God's will, and it's help-ful to understand the distinctions. What some theologians call God's *revealed* will is what He has shown us in the Bible about His character and desires. If you are praying toward something that the Scriptures clearly spell out as a worthy prayer target, go for it! But if you are praying about doing something you know is sin, save your breath—if you are ask-ing God to violate His character or His commands in any way, you're wasting your time. If you aren't sure if something is God's revealed will, do a thorough Bible study and ask your pastor for help.

If you can't come up with an answer, then you may be dealing with what theologians sometimes call God's *permissive* will—situations He has not specifically addressed in His Word. For example, does God want you to pray about your brother's promotion at work?

Likely, yes. Does God want to give your brother the promotion? If you have heard from the Lord clearly to pray for your brother's promotion, you can do so with great assurance and confidence until you sense a "release" from your praying in this regard. Otherwise, unless you can find your brother's name in your Bible (and I don't mean in the family tree inside the front cover!) you don't *know* for certain. Can God provide that promotion? No doubt about it! So you pray for your brother's promotion, believing that God can provide it and asking that He will do so. If He provides it, Jesus gets the praise and glory—your prayer is answered. If He doesn't, it's because He has chosen not to—at least at this time—and that's your answer as well.

There are times when I hear from God very clearly about a prayer target and can pray accordingly. At other times I don't hear so clearly but I ask anyway. If I get a check in my spirit about the praying, or if I lose the impetus to do it, I consider *that* my answer and back off until the Lord leads otherwise.

Experience and biblical precedent show that God would like to do *a whole lot more* than He does—we just need to ask! Bottom line: God answers prayer. He is ready to do far beyond our wildest dreams if we will ask. A. W. Tozer sums this up quite succinctly: "The truth is that God always answers the prayer that accords with His will as revealed in the Scriptures, provided the one who prays is obedient and trustful."[8]

Why is prayer so hard?

Well, prayer isn't hard for everybody. God has given some folks the ability to excel in intercessory prayer; these are the people who get up in the morning, head to the prayer closet, and emerge one to four hours later—every day. They aren't super-spiritual; they are just wired that way. But that is not an excuse for those of us who aren't wired that way to slack off in our praying. The "closet pray-ers" would say that their praying is hard, too, just on a different level from the rest of us.

Prayer can be hard, but like most spiritual disciplines (Scripture reading, memorization and meditation, fasting, giving, and so on) one gets better at it with practice and perseverance. Exercising our spiritual muscles in prayer improves our stamina; it also helps our ability to concentrate. Most of us have struggled with this: We are praying for something or somebody, and ten minutes later we discover, to our dismay, we have thought about at least a dozen different subjects, none of which are related to our praying. This does not need to be a life-long struggle! Growth and improvement will come with time, and before you know it you will be entering into an intimacy with the Father that you never could have imagined. The disciples asked Jesus, "Lord, teach us to pray" (Luke 11:1). It's a good idea to make that request our own!

Do we need to pray about everything?

Recently I ordered a new laptop computer to replace my old, beat-up one. A few days after placing the order, I realized that available finances to pay for it had evaporated. Oops. Then I found out that because the computer had been special ordered, I couldn't cancel the order. If you guessed I didn't pray much about the purchase, you guessed right. I then placed an ad in the local paper, thinking I would sell it to a private party and absorb a relatively small loss on the transaction. I *did* pray that God would provide a buyer (I'm a quick learner). When I immediately received an inquiry, I completed the transaction and considered the mishap a good learning experience.

But my consideration was premature; nine days after the transaction, my bank sent a notice saying that the cashier's check I had received as payment was counterfeit. I immediately called the phone number I had used to complete the transaction. The person on the other end claimed to have no idea what I was talking about, insisting that he had *not* purchased a computer from me. I guess I'm not *that* quick of a learner—the moment the initial phone call came from the interested party, my prayers ended on this matter. The mishap ended up being a good yet *costly* learning experience! If I had prayed, would I have known not to order the computer, or to sell it to a bogus buyer? I don't know for sure, but I could have known that God was "in" what transpired, whatever that might have been.

My point is that "praying continually"[9] (1 Thessalonians 5:17—the *New American Standard Bible* translates this as "pray without ceasing") is not idealistic, but an attainable goal! There are times when we are to engage in the kind of focused intercession that obviously can't take place when we are engaged in other activities. But our goal should be to develop our intimacy with the Father to the extent that we are engaging in what Brother Lawrence called "practicing the presence of God."[10] And when we are "practicing," our thoughts become more and more His thoughts, and our prayers become more and more His prayers.

When I was in seminary, I had a classmate who we affectionately called "Praying Karl." Karl would pray over the drinking fountain before he took a drink! Back then we thought Karl was going overboard with the prayer thing. Today, though I have no idea what Karl was praying about, I'm not so sure he was going overboard—the rest of us were more likely "underboard" (if that's a word) concerning prayer.

Keep looking for answers.

There are many more legitimate questions that can surface concerning prayer. I have only tried to tackle the ones that, in my experience, are asked most often. Sometimes our failure to grow mighty in the area of prayer is not because we need better ideas, but because we need better theology. We also need to establish some solid praying practices, including listening.

Notes

1. I'm sure this movie, which was released in 1989, did not coin the phrase *Carpe Diem*—Latin for "seize the day"—but the lead character, played by Robin Williams, surely branded it on the public consciousness, as evidenced by the run of Carpe Diem coffee mugs, coasters, wall plaques, and assorted other paraphernalia in the ensuing years. *Carpe diem gloria Deo*—*Seize the day for the glory of God*—is my Christian version. If my Latin grammar is not perfect, I ask forgiveness in advance (which I know is not good theology, but you get the point).

2. I think it was Pascal who said this, but I can't seem to find out for certain. I have tried to be a good journalist, but you're going to find a few more of these "somebody said" style quotes in the pages that follow, where I tried to track down the sources to no avail.

3. I am assuming we all realize that prayer is not the sole means of cultivating a relationship with God.

4. Richard Foster, *Prayer: Finding the Heart's True Home* (San Francisco, Calif.: HarperCollins, 1992), pp. 180-181.

5. Dutch Sheets, *Intercessory Prayer* (Ventura, Calif.: Regal Books, 1996), pp. 28-29.

6. C. Peter Wagner, *Confronting the Powers* (Ventura, Calif.: Regal Books, 1996), p. 242 as quoted in Dutch Sheet's *Intercessory Prayer*.

7. Jack Hayford, *Prayer Is Invading the Impossible*, (South Plainfield, N.J.: Logos International, 1977), p. 92.

8. A. W. Tozer, *Man: The Dwelling Place of God* (Camp Hill, Pa: Christian Publications, 1966), Chapter 21.

9. Paul expands on this short phrase in his epistle to the Ephesians: "And pray in the Spirit on all occasions with all kinds of prayers and requests. With this in mind, be alert and always keep on praying for all the saints" (6:18).

10. The classic by Brother Lawrence, *The Practice of the Presence of God*, was written in the 1600s and is considered one of the top Christian books of all time.

3. UNCUT DIAMONDS: UNITED PRAYER AND LISTENING PRAYER

There has never been a spiritual awakening in any country or locality that did not begin in united prayer.

—A. T. Pierson

God is not a silent friend. He longs to speak to us; however, we often do not hear His voice because we are too busy talking ourselves.

—Elizabeth Alves

When the courtship of my bride turned serious, we began talking about diamonds. It wasn't as in, "How big of a diamond would you like?" or, "Will you need a sling for your arm when I slip that boulder on your finger?" We talked more hypothetically, in the coy manner of two lovebirds that had not yet taken the leap: "Well, if we were to get engaged and if that engagement included a ring, would you want a diamond on that ring?" Terri was pretty adamant about preferring a simple gold band, sans diamond. But I was "old school," so when somebody donated a diamond to our church, I figured my bride-to-be was gonna get a rock (or, more accurately, a pebble). If she didn't want it on her ring, she could wear it around her neck or wherever. The appraisal of the diamond showed it to be affordable to me, but before I paid for it, I wanted to know what I was buying. I had no clue what four of the five Cs of diamond evaluation meant (color, clarity, cut, and carat; I did figure out cost), so I did my homework. In that process, I was reminded that diamonds don't come out of the ground all sparkling and beautiful. As a matter of fact, they look rather unremarkable in their natural condition. However, when they are cut and refined, it is an entirely different matter.

There are many aspects of prayer that are likely worthy of their own chapters. Richard Foster, in his seminal work, *Prayer: Finding the Heart's True Home*, identifies twenty-one dimensions of prayer and devotes a chapter to each one.[1] Yet I believe united prayer and listening prayer are two of the more valuable "uncut diamonds" in the prayer jewel collection, especially in the context of the practice of prayer in youth ministry. I call them so because they often have not been "cut" so that their full beauty and value is on display. But when they are cut, when proper attention is given to them in the context of the full spectrum of prayer, they refract and reflect the light of the Father in an especially unique way. They are often underutilized if not neglected, and occasionally misunderstood. Yet they are among the more strategic types of prayer when it comes to reaching emerging generations of youth for Christ. So much so, that in my opinion, they warrant a closer examination.

United Prayer

Almost all of us have some experience praying with others. This kind of prayer takes place during church worship services, before and after (sometimes during) youth group meetings, during youth staff gatherings, in small groups with kids, and in a variety of other situations. If you grew up in a Christian home, praying with others was likely a component of your family devotional time. But there is a subtle, yet important, distinction between simply praying with others—corporate prayer—and united prayer. United prayer takes place only when those in the group or corporate setting are in agreement about the subject of their praying. In characterizing the early church, Acts 1:14 (KJV) uses the phrase "with one accord" to describe the disciples praying together. They are all asking God for the same thing.

While some may consider effective corporate prayer to consist of gathering the numerical prerequisite described in Matthew 18:19-20, the fact that this passage stresses agreement makes it clear that not just corporate prayer, but united prayer is where the power lies:

> "Again, I tell you that if two of you on earth agree about anything you ask for, it will be done for you by my Father in heaven. For where two or three come together in my name, there am I with them."

When the pastor is praying in a church service, there is hopefully a measure of united prayer happening simultaneously. But it is probably also safe to assume that at least some are not tuned in to the pastor's prayer. A few may even be snoozing! The same is probably true when it comes to group prayer in our youth ministries—kids are thinking about homework, the big game, an attractive member of the other gender, whatever.

When I was in college, a group from my fraternity used to meet regularly at 6:30 a.m. for united prayer. One morning, I decided to pray from a facedown position, being the pious man that I am. I awoke at 9 a.m. in a dark, empty room, having missed my first two classes. I might have met the "gathered" criteria, but I sure hadn't met the "agreement" clause!

Effective united prayer is not always that easy to achieve. Many of the same struggles that we deal with in our personal prayer lives—drowsiness, wandering thoughts, daydreaming—are present. And to further complicate things, if we are not the person doing the praying, we need to mentally follow along with that person so that we can agree with the prayer. That is not always easy to do if the pray-er gets verbose or gets off the subject. And if we're in a setting where several folks are praying, our mental acuity must be on high alert, because "pray-like-a-child" may be followed by "pray-like-a-theologian," "pray-like-King-James," "pray-to-inform-God," and "pray-all-over-the-place." Now *that* can be a challenge! But it is a challenge that pays huge dividends. Further explanation is in order here.

It is becoming increasingly apparent that if the church is to fulfill its mission on earth, the petty jealousies, arguments, and enmity that have often existed among us (in the forms of denominationalism, nonessential theology disputes, turf battles, and so on) must come to an end. It's pretty clear that loving one another (John 13:35) and unity (John 17) were of paramount importance to Jesus, who implied that our greatest apologetic will be more than how well we can articulate the gospel message or how culturally relevant our ministry programs may be; rather, it will be how well we get along with each other. I believe that one of the reasons this is so is that love and unity are reflections of the character of the trinity; that the Father, Son, and Holy Spirit incarnate, in the truest sense of the word *unity*, express love and unity (see Deuteronomy 6:4; 1 John 4:7-8). As the church relationally and incarnationally demonstrates love and unity to the world, we reflect the character of the trinity and, according to John 17:23, validate Christ as the Son of God.

Most of us would readily concur that love and unity are a big deal to God. We would also acknowledge that the church has, for the most part, messed up our display of love and unity to an unbelieving world. And, if we thought about it, we would agree that unity is not the same as unanimity (agreeing about *everything*) or uniformity (becoming one big, homogeneous church). But if unity is not unanimity or uniformity, then what is it? A good analogy here is the process of making wine. Simply put, wine is the result of grapes being smashed together until their skins burst and the inner juices are released to flow together. Similarly, as members of the body of Christ in a particular community, when we position ourselves together to allow the Holy Spirit to break down our walls and crush us together, so to speak, then the new wine flows and those in the community who taste it respond,

"Hey, this is excellent!" The precursor to the making of this "new wine" is getting the grapes together, which puts a premium on relationships.

Relationships are the context in which love and unity are defined and explored. Relationships allow trust to be established and developed within the body of Christ, no matter what denominational or nonessential theological differences may be. When this happens, when the walls start to come down between us, we have new freedom to be honest with ourselves and with each other. Only then is the Holy Spirit able to intensify the process of dissolving those "walls"—the stuff that keeps us from being clean before God and right with one another, and hinders our efforts to be light and salt in our communities—that impede unity. And in the context of this unity, we are able to experience a greater measure of trinitarian love, expressed through Christ:

> For this reason I kneel before the Father, from whom his whole family in heaven and on earth derives its name. I pray that out of his glorious riches he may strengthen you with power through his Spirit in your inner being, so that Christ may dwell in your hearts through faith. And I pray that you, being rooted and established in love, may have power, together with all the saints, to grasp how wide and long and high and deep is the love of Christ, and to know this love that surpasses knowledge—that you may be filled to the measure of all the fullness of God.
> —Ephesians 3:14-19

Mac Pier comments on this prayer written by the Apostle Paul for the Ephesian believers:

> We can't do it alone. We can't fully experience the love of God in isolation. If there is no other reason to unite with others in prayer, this is the reason. If you want to experience the love of Christ in all its fullness, you must be united with other believers. It is not optional—it is imperative.[2]

Loving unity (unity that is loving) is powerful stuff! And united prayer is a wonderfully practical representation of this love and unity. This kind of prayer, in the context of biblical "one-another" style relationships, is an extension of the intimate trinitarian expression of love and unity for which we were created. As such, it receives divine impetus, sanction, and blessing:

> How good and pleasant it is when brothers live together in unity! It is like precious oil poured on the head, running down on the beard, running down on Aaron's beard, down upon the collar of his robes. It is as if the dew of Hermon were falling on Mount Zion. For there the LORD bestows his blessing, even life forevermore.
>
> —Psalm 133

In Matthew 18:19-20, which we referred to earlier, Jesus makes it clear that united prayer packs some unusual power.

The early church certainly put this teaching into practice. Following Jesus' ascension in Acts 1, the small band of disciples "all joined together constantly in prayer" (1:14).[3] Following Pentecost, the early church was characterized as being devoted to corporate prayer (2:42). United prayer was their response to Peter and John's initial run-in with the Sanhedrin (4:24-30). Peter's release from Herod's imprisonment was the direct result of united prayer (12:5-14).

Not only is united prayer powerful, but it is also something in which anyone can participate. The beauty of the metaphor concerning Christ's body in 1 Corinthians 12 is certainly operative in united prayer: neophyte and seasoned intercessors, those who are comfortable praying out loud and those who have rarely done so, can all agree together in prayer. The power in such united prayer is not in the eloquence, fervency, or theology of those praying, but in the Matthew 18-style agreement. United prayer can, obviously, take place in a host of venues—anywhere two or more gather in His name. Such prayer can be a wonderful classroom experience for those desiring to ascend on their own prayer learning curve.

Listening Prayer

Let me return to the wooing of my bride for a minute. One of the pivotal points in our journey from courtship to engagement had to do with communication. During our premarital counseling, we were required to read *Communication: Key to Your Marriage* by H. Norman Wright. Our counselors realized how important communication—specifically, two-way communication—was to a healthy marital relationship. But in the earlier stages of our courtship, I hadn't read the book, didn't understand this "key," and had placed the future of our relationship in peril because *I was a crummy listener.* Terri didn't feel like she was being heard, and it was her courage in voicing that concern that gave me a much-needed wake-up call.

Similarly, many of us in youth ministry need a "wake-up call" to discover the uncut diamond of listening prayer. We need to be reminded that communication—make that two-way communication—is just as much a key to our relationship with God as it is to a marriage relationship, or any other relationship for that matter. Our prayer lives often consist of too much time talking to God and asking Him for things, and too little time spent listening to what He might have to say to us. More of us are familiar with the story of Samuel, who after originally mistaking God's voice for that of Eli, assumed a listening posture: "Then Samuel said, 'Speak, for your servant is listening'" (1 Samuel 3:10). More convicting to me is the following passage: "Guard your steps when you go to the house of God. Go near to *listen* rather than to offer the sacrifice of fools, who do not know that they do wrong" (Ecclesiastes 5:1, emphasis mine).

One of the many reasons I consider listening prayer to be an uncut diamond is that youth workers (I include myself here) are notorious for making great plans, then asking God to bless those plans, rather than seeking Him for His plans in the first place. Here's an example: Most good youth workers base what they are doing on a vision statement, which Dennis Miller defines as "discerning, understanding, and living God's desires for your life and ministry direction."[4] Some would call this a mission statement, but regardless, the thrust is similar.

It is important to have a good vision or mission statement. The problem is that too often, our vision is the by-product of things other than *what God has revealed to us.* We give priority to what we think our kids will like, or what the book written by the guy with five thousand kids in his youth group says, or what the senior pastor and parents expect. When that happens, we too often end up stuck in a ministry program cycle described by Miller:

Program
> Initial excitement
>> Novelty wanes
>>> Excitement replaced by responsibility
>>> Other interests
>>>> New, improved program (or burnout)
>>>> Initial excitement
>>>>> (etc.—Repeat cycle)[5]

I have been trapped in this cycle enough to know how debilitating it can be over time. As you can imagine, the cycle is broken only when the youth worker packs up and moves on, gets "moved on," or burns out. The problem here is not necessarily the program—we do need programs. The problem lies in our lack of confidence that our strategy is God-given and custom-tailored by the Holy Spirit for us, our ministry, and for our time. If our program or ministry strategy is a product of inquiring of the Lord, and if we are continually seeking Him concerning what changes, adjustments, or fine-tuning we need to implement, we will grow confident in what we are doing. We will persevere when the novelty wanes (and it will) and when criticism comes (and it will, too). We will be flexible—willing to adjust and change what we are doing as the Spirit leads. And we will experience the blessing of obedience. Otherwise, entrapment in the program cycle is inevitable.

This is just one ministry-oriented example of the benefits and blessings of listening prayer. God *does* speak today. He has always spoken and continues to do so—corporately and individually. Most of us realize that He speaks to us through His Word, through other believers, through His creation, and sometimes through circumstances. What we often fail to realize is that He also speaks to us Spirit to spirit. What the champions of the faith throughout the ages have called the "still, small voice" speaks to us even today. The problem is, we often have not developed the spiritual ears to hear His voice. The experience of the church since New Testament times is that God usually does not speak to us in an audible voice, but His divine whisper can be recognized if we have attuned our ears to hear.

In the Old Testament, the biblical model for this listening type of prayer is often called "inquiring of the LORD." David did it all the time (see 1 Samuel 30:8; 2 Samuel 2:1, 5:19,23) as did Jehoshaphat (see 1 Kings 22:7-8; 2 Kings 3:11; 2 Chronicles 20). But the most telling passages to me describe the results of failing to do so. Here are several examples of how God dealt with the leaders, kings, and His everyday folks when they failed to inquire of Him.

First example: King Saul got booted from his position and bit the dust because he was clueless when it came to listening to God.

> Saul died because he was unfaithful to the LORD; he did not keep the word of the LORD and even consulted a medium for guidance, and did not inquire of the LORD. So the LORD put him to death and turned the kingdom over to David son of Jesse.
>
> —1 Chronicles 10:13-14

Example two: God warned the Israelites—and then punished them—time after time for turning from listening to Him, which caused them to repeatedly sin.

> I will stretch out my hand against Judah and against all who live in Jerusalem. . . . I will cut off those who turn back from following the LORD and neither seek the LORD nor inquire of him.
>
> —Zephaniah 1:4,6

Example three: During the time when the kingdom of Israel was divided into a northern kingdom of Israel and a southern kingdom of Judah, there were a series of corrupt kings and leadership teams who did not inquire of God. They turned from listening to God to listening to idols and foreign rulers. God, in His mercy, sent prophet after prophet to warn the rulers and people of impending judgment. Sometimes God's people listened and repented. Wise move. At other times, they did not.

Elijah brought bad news to King Ahaziah of Judah because the king consulted the idol of foreigners.

> [The prophet Elijah] told the king [Ahaziah], "This is what the LORD says: Is it because there is no God in Israel for you to consult that you have sent messengers to consult Baal-Zebub, the god of Ekron? Because you have done this, you will never leave the bed you are lying on. You will certainly die!" So he died, according to the word of the LORD that Elijah had spoken.
>
> —2 Kings 1:16-17

Likewise, Shemaiah prophesied doom for King Rehoboam and all the leaders of Judah. God had mercy on them when they humbled themselves before Him.

> Because they had been unfaithful to the LORD, Shishak king of Egypt attacked Jerusalem in the fifth year of King Rehoboam. . . . Then the prophet Shemaiah came to Rehoboam and to the leaders of Judah who had assembled in Jerusalem for fear of Shishak, and he said to them, "This is what the LORD says, 'You have abandoned me; therefore, I now abandon you to Shishak.'"

The leaders of Israel and the king humbled themselves and said, "The LORD is just."

When the LORD saw that they humbled themselves, this word of the LORD came to Shemaiah: "Since they have humbled themselves, I will not destroy them but will soon give them deliverance. My wrath will not be poured out on Jerusalem through Shishak. They will, however, become subject to him, so that they may learn the difference between serving me and serving the kings of other lands. . . ."

Because Rehoboam humbled himself, the LORD's anger turned from him, and he was not totally destroyed. Indeed, there was some good in Judah.

—2 Chronicles 12:2,5-8,12

God has a strategy for each youth group, youth ministry network, and city movement. That includes *yours*! Your primary means of discovering that strategy is listening to God. What works in my youth ministry may not work in yours. What works in my town will not necessarily work in your town. Certainly there are transferable principles of ministry. But I am convinced that *inquiring of the Lord and listening to His voice* is critical to the release of divine strategy that will make the kind of localized, transformational impact upon the youth that so many of us pray to see.

You may ask, "Mike, how can I tell if God is speaking to me?" I wish I could say that there is a cut-and-dried formula for discerning His voice, but honestly, the only way I can tell if God is speaking to me is that I *know* it is Him. I don't always *know* with absolute certainty. There are often competing voices for my attention—my own busy mind and the enemy being two of the more prominent ones—yet often my spirit bears witness that what I am hearing is, indeed, God speaking. He also speaks to us in different ways, probably according to our ability to hear—through prayer and meditation, wise counsel from others, Scripture, and how He has ordered our circumstances.

My wife has the "big dish" of reception in hearing the Lord's voice, and it is a common experience for her to hear from God. She makes ample time in her devotions for listening, and she has recorded page after page in her journal of things He has said to her. I try to do likewise, but as of yet have not had the same measure of success. (My "receptor" is more of a radio antenna than a dish!) God often speaks to me in what I call "dictation." During the course of the day (or sometimes in the middle of the night) I will have this spiritual awareness that God has something to say to me, so I pull out pen and paper and start writing. I keep both items handy at my bedside for this reason. Frequently God also speaks to me through His Word in typical Bible-study methods such as observation, interpretation, and personal application. There are also times when I am reading a passage of Scripture and it seems as though the words are directed at me personally. You've experienced that from time to time, haven't you? At times God speaks to me by impressing a Scripture reference on my mind, which I may or may not be familiar with, and when I turn there I find it is *exactly* what I needed to hear in that season. This, to me, is cool stuff!

While inquiring of the Lord is crucial, I need to interject something here that is even more necessary. There is a subtle but important distinction between *inquiring* of the Lord and *seeking* the Lord. God's foremost desire is that we come to Him primarily for who He *is* to us rather than for what He *does* for us. Thus, *seeking* should take precedence over the inquiring. "Seeking His face" (a common biblical injunction with an emphasis on relationship) should take priority over "seeking His hand" of blessing:

One thing I ask of the LORD, this is what I seek: that I may dwell in the house of the LORD all the days of my life, to gaze upon the beauty of the LORD and to seek him in his temple . . . .
My heart says of you, "Seek his face!" Your face, LORD, I will seek.

—Psalm 27:4,8

O God, you are my God, earnestly I seek you; my soul thirsts for you, my body longs for you, in a dry and weary land where there is no water.

—Psalm 63:1

For David and other biblical witnesses, seeking that relationship with God was of paramount importance. Inquiring of Him was important—the danger of myopically seeking yet not inquiring was (and is) very real—but the *relationship* was top priority. This should be the case for us in youth ministry.

My desire is for my children to love me more for who I *am* to them as their father than for what I *do* for them as their parental vending machine. I'm sure our heavenly Father feels the same way about us. Our kids are usually more interested in the immediate things we can do for them; as they grow older, we pray they will place more emphasis on who we are to them. Similarly, God understands our requests for Him to do things for us and is honored when we look to Him as our provider. Yet as we seek Him and worship Him alone, focusing on *being* His child before *doing* His work (think Mary vs. Martha), we greatly please the God who is more concerned about who we are *to Him* than what we do *for Him*.

Notes

1. Note the chapters in Foster's book you might find helpful for follow-up: Simple Prayer; Prayer of the Forsaken; The Prayer of Examen; The Prayer of Tears; The Prayer of Relinquishment; Formation Prayer; Covenant Prayer; The Prayer of Adoration; The Prayer of Rest; Sacramental Prayer; Unceasing Prayer; The Prayer of the Heart; Meditative Prayer; Praying the Ordinary; Petitionary Prayer; Intercessory Prayer; Healing Prayer; The Prayer of Suffering; Authoritative Prayer; Radical Prayer. (Whew!)
2. Mac Pier and Katie Sweeting, *The Power of a City at Prayer* (Downers Grove, Ill.: InterVarsity. 2002). p. 125.

3. It is important to note that the early church practiced not only united prayer, but also united worship: "And they stayed continually at the temple, praising God" (Luke 24:53).
4. Dennis Miller, *Changing Lives: A Practical Guide to a Spiritually Powerful Youth Ministry* (Shakopee, Minn.: CD Books, 1988), p. 100.
5. Miller, p. 95.

PART II: THE PRAYING YOUTH WORKER

4. REIMAGINING YOUTH MINISTRY— AND YOUTH MINISTERS

What the church needs today is not more machinery or better, not new organizations or more and novel methods, but men whom the Holy Spirit can use—men of prayer, men mighty in prayer.

—E. M. Bounds

Q: How many youth workers does it take to change a lightbulb?
A: Youth workers aren't around long enough for a lightbulb to burn out.

In my early years of youth work, a commonly quoted statistic was that the average tenure of a vocational youth worker at a church was sixteen months. As of late, I have heard revised numbers of up to twenty-four months (time to party!), although I haven't had any better success tracking down the source of the current figure than I did tracking down the old one. Both might be, to an extent, youth ministry legends. But over the years, I have heard very few dispute either figure. Even if both figures are off 50 percent or more, it's still a pathetic commentary. These are great statistics to share when exhorting youth workers to perseverance, or challenging churches and ministries to make the care and nurture of their youth worker a higher priority. But what's behind the statistics? Why is the turnover so high in youth ministry? Why is it such a challenge for youth workers to stay planted in one locale? And I'm sure you are asking, "What's all this have to do with prayer?" It has everything to do with prayer, as we will soon see.

There are myriad reasons for such a high rate of youth worker turnover—low pay, long hours, unrealistic expectations, conflicts with parents and senior pastors, and so on. Often, the problem lies not with the ministry, but rather with the minister. Two news reports recently surfaced in my community concerning ministers who were arrested for sexual impropriety—one of the two worked with youth. I'm not sure that moral default is a leading cause of attrition among youth workers, but if I had a dollar for every incident I have heard about over the years, my ministry would be close to endowed.

The reports came to my attention soon after I came across two provocative articles in a youth ministry journal. Mike Yaconelli wrote about "The Failure of Youth Ministry," and concluded, "Youth ministry as an experiment has failed. If we want to see the church survive, we need to rethink youth ministry."[1] Dan Kimball's article in the same publication asked, "Do We Need Youth Ministry Anymore?" He wrote, "So, do we still need youth ministry? Yes, but we need to re-imagine it. We don't need to throw it all away, just rethink what we do and what we need to do. . . . Youth pastors and youth leaders must lead the way in this reimagining."[2]

I liked much of what these two had to say about our need to rethink or re-imagine youth ministry if we are going to reach and disciple emerging generations of youth. But I contend that our reimagining must start at a deeper level—reimagining of youth *workers*. Certainly, our youth ministry methodology could use an overhaul. But the most culturally-relevant, family-oriented, biblically-based youth ministry philosophy in the world won't matter if it is led by folks who have a propensity for ministry burnout or moral and ethical failure.

So how do we go about "reimagining" youth workers? My contention is that today, a re-imagined youth worker is one who has made the paradigm shift that Bob Sorge describes as a transformation from "a worker who loves, to a lover who works." Reflect on that statement for a minute, because it's much more than mere play on words. Sorge elaborates:

> The overriding paradigm being modeled in the church today is that of the servant, the worker who loves. . . . But God is changing this. The revelation of Christ as our Bridegroom will awaken us to our identity first and foremost as lovers of God. The flame of that passion will in turn ignite the greatest labors for the Kingdom.[3]

If we are honest, we will admit that most of us fit in the "worker who loves" category. We tend to be defined by what we do as youth "workers" more than by who we are: members of the Bride of Christ, lovesick for our Bridegroom. We have a whole lot of Martha in us and not nearly enough Mary.

So how do we make this paradigm shift from a worker who loves to a lover who works? This question requires a more complex answer. One of the more common biblical models of reimagining is a "God-encounter." Abram became Abraham through a God-encounter. Jacob became Israel in a similar fashion, as did Saul, who became Paul. Those name changes are not insignificant. There are others who kept their names—Moses, Job, Isaiah, Ezekiel, and John among them—who also were re-imagined (i.e., transformed) through a God-encounter. The point is not the name change; rather, it is the encounter.

For some of us today, sometimes a God-encounter is a singular, goose bump-producing event that rocks our world and leaves our faces metaphorically glowing in the dark. Yet perhaps for most of us, our encounter is a process through which God reveals Himself to us, day by day, through His Word, prayer, and other disciplines of grace in new and wonderful ways. Christ becomes a longed-for Bridegroom, and we in turn become lovers who work, through the disciplines of daily living.

It is in the crucible of daily living where our need for each other is apparent. We need fellow guides, encouragers, exhorters, and confessors as we engage in this reimagining process—a postmodern pursuit of holiness—because there are a number of formidable obstacles along the way:

- **Ruined relationships.** We need help to keep from neglecting spouses and children, and to strengthen the *quality* of our relationships and the *quantity* of our time we spend with them.
- **Raunchy recreation.** Youth workers can harm their own hearts by ingesting impure material from the Internet (porn), movies, magazines, music, and other media. Sure, we need to connect with the culture. But the purity of our hearts is more precious than the garbage we say we're viewing in order to stay cutting-edge. Let's help each other in this.
- **Rude rappin'.** Stuff that is considered not *really* bad and has been deemed acceptable by some youth workers because it is "edgy"—dirty jokes, other unwholesome talk, coarse jesting and the like—comes out of the mouths of youth workers. The biblical admonition, "Nor should there be obscenity, foolish talk, or coarse jesting" (Ephesians 5:4) must be taken literally.
- **Rotten refreshment.** Obesity, caffeine addiction, and daily donut breakfasts do not refresh! Exercise, healthy eating, and self-control do! Abuse of my physical body has had more of a negative impact on my ministry effectiveness than any slipping of spiritual disciplines or lack of ministry training. We need each other to help guard the health of our physical bodies. Healthy bodies enhance our ability to think and pray clearly, deal with stress, and survive those seasons of youth ministry when schedules go amok.

We need each other's help in other ways:

- **Reconciliation.** We need each other's help to guard against broken relationships, unresolved conflict, and letting the sun go down on our anger (Ephesians 4:26). If we are harboring anger or bitterness toward anyone, be it a student, parent, senior pastor, fellow youth worker, spouse, or child, we have given the devil a foothold in our lives (Ephesians 4:27). That is not a good thing! Someone said, "If you let the devil in the car, he's gonna eventually want to drive."

- **Rushing.** We need each other's help to guard our devotional/prayer time. The tyranny of the urgent *will* strike and we *will* be tempted to cut back on our time with the Lord so we can get more done—a practice that does not really make a lot of sense, does it? We need to be periodically reminded of this (at least I do).
- **Rapprochement.** Defined by Webster as bringing together and establishing "cordial relationship." We need each other's help not only to ask hard questions and maintain a high level of accountability, but also to provide encouragement, positive feedback, affirmation, and blessing. The sad but true fact is that often we're not going to get much of that from youth, or parents, or even some senior pastors.

If we are to drastically reduce the numbers of defaulting youth workers, and if we are going to successfully re-imagine youth ministry *and* youth ministers, we need each other's abiding support in a safe, grace-filled environment. This is a great apologetic for relationship-based youth worker networking, isn't it? But let's go beyond that to a deeper level. In each of the bulleted statements above another word can easily be substituted for *each other*: We need *God.* And if we need God, then similarly, we need *prayer.* As vitally important as youth worker networking is, the reimagining transformation from "youth worker who loves God" to "lover of God who does youth work" must involve a parallel transformation in our prayer lives.

Once we make the paradigm shift from workers who love to lovers who work, and once we realize that a parallel transformation in our prayer lives is necessary, then we can begin the process of upgrading our prayer lives.

Notes

1. Mike Yaconelli, "The Failure of Youth Ministry," *Youthworker Journal*, May/June 2003, p. 64.
2. Dan Kimball, "Do We Need Youth Ministry Anymore?" *Youthworker Journal*, May/June 2003, p. 16.
3. Bob Sorge, *Pain, Perplexity and Promotion* (Greenwood, Mo: Oasis House, 2002), p. 174.

5. UPGRADING YOUR PRAYER LIFE

This is the only way we shall ever learn to pray, by just beginning to do it. And as the babbling child learns the art of speech by speaking, and the lark mounts up to the heights of the sky by beating its little wings again and again upon the air, so prayer will teach us how to pray; and the more we pray, the more shall we learn the mysteries, and heights, and depths of prayer.

—A. B. Simpson

I was a wet-behind-the-ears leader of a fledgling prayer ministry who somehow found himself at a national prayer consultation in Colorado, and I was accelerating along my learning curve so quickly that the G-forces were making me dizzy. I was a nobody from "Or-y-gun" and one of the very few youth workers in a gathering of hundreds who for the most part led national or international prayer ministries and movements. But the wealth of information, inspiration, and impartation was off the charts for me. So for those three days I morphed into a human sponge and did my best to absorb anything and everything.

During one session, we were encouraged to join with two others to form "prayer trip-lets" for a time of intercession. Without giving it a whole lot of thought, I turned my chair around and found myself in a group with Evelyn Christenson and Bobbie Byerly. You may not recognize those names, but it was the prayer ministry equivalent of sitting down with champion golfers Jack Nicklaus and Tiger Woods . . . or evangelists Billy Graham and Luis Palau . . . or basketball greats Michael Jordan and Tim Duncan . . . . or television titans Oprah Winfrey and Barbara Walters . . . or country music legends Willie Nelson and Johnny Cash (ok, I got carried away). Now, sitting down with them was intimidating enough, but I was going to have to *pray* with them. Tiger was going to hand me the driver and say, "You tee off first!"

To be honest, I have little recollection of how our time of intercession transpired. I do remember that Evelyn and Bobbie didn't appear to waste a whole lot of brain energy wondering who this guy sitting with them was, or if he could hold his own in united prayer (I couldn't, but they didn't know that). They just started praying, I went along for the ride, and I walked away having learned two important insights concerning prayer.

Somebody once said, "Ninety percent of success is just showing up." Well, the first thing I learned is that 90 percent of effective praying is just showing up to do it. Eloquence is not the issue — Evelyn and Bobbie certainly prayed with a passion and intimacy that was unfamiliar to me at the time, but it wasn't like they were praying Beethoven's Ninth Symphony while I was praying "Chopsticks." Volume is not important (God is not hard of hearing), nor is using King James English. What is important is that you are doing it, that you just show up and participate, be it in a corporate setting or in your own prayer closet.

The second thing I learned is that the best way to grow in prayer is to surround yourself with praying people. Somebody else once said, "Prayer is better caught than taught,"[1] and after spending more than a decade around a number of world-class prayer warriors, I wholeheartedly concur. That was just as true for me in my infancy in Christ. I came to Christ at age eighteen, and up to that time my prayer repertoire consisted of grace over meals and a bedtime prayer. I learned early on that "The LORD does not look at the things man looks at. Man looks at the outward appearance, but the LORD looks at the heart" (1 Samuel 16:7). Yet despite a well-intending heart, I had no clue how to start, how to finish, what to pray about, how long to pray, and so on.

I got great resources in my discipleship group. (Most of my generation is intimately familiar with The Navigators' hand and wheel illustrations, which are invaluable teaching visuals.) But I learned the most by *listening to others pray.* Evelyn and Bobbie weren't in my college fellowship, but Dan, Phil, Jerry, and Tom were. They were among the first of myriad prayer mentors I have acquired over the years.

There is a third important thing I have learned concerning prayer, and I certainly didn't learn it from Evelyn and Bobbie. I learned it the hard way. I write these words with literal fear and trembling, because I do not want to be misunderstood. What I have learned through my own lengthy struggles is that the key to an effective personal prayer life is not passion, or persistence, or patience, or perseverance. Those are all important, and I could give you chapter and verse in support of them all. But I believe the key to intimacy with the Father and a quantum-upgraded prayer life is *purity.* Here is where the fear and trembling kick in: My experience as an observer/participant in youth ministry over several decades has shown that purity may not be one of our greatest strengths as youth workers.

I know many youth workers who keep really short accounts with God. I could provide a long list—many names on it would be quite familiar to you—of men and women of God who work with youth and from what I can tell are as pure as the driven snow. I am not the chief of the purity police—far from it, considering my own battles in this area—and I cannot (nor will I) judge the hearts of the brothers and sisters I love so dearly. But is there a connection between the lack of power in our prayer and the purity of our hearts? As we seek to mentor kids in the arena of prayer, do we fail to place enough emphasis on the importance of purity? I think so.

I must take some time to define what I mean by purity, so we don't restrict the definition to moral or sexual varieties, as important as they are. Psalm 24 has been the theme of a number of younger generation-oriented gatherings of the past several years. I believe this is not coincidental, so let's take a closer look at the passage. Some commentators think the psalm to be a processional liturgy composed for the occasion when David first brought the ark to Jerusalem.

That story, found in 2 Samuel 6, is one of my favorites. David was desperate to get the ark of God to recently captured Jerusalem, which he was establishing as the capital city of Israel. He didn't just want the ark there as an artifact from the days of Moses. He wanted what dwelled in between the cherubim on the top of the ark—the presence of God. He wanted God's presence as close as possible, both for him personally and for the people of his city and nation. So he assembled a small contingent—thirty thousand chosen men—and headed to Abinadab's shack to fetch it. That is where the ark had resided since the Philistines, who captured it years previously and subsequently saw their cities of Ashdod and Ekron devastated (see 1 Samuel 4–5), panicked and returned it in a hurry (1 Samuel 6:1–7:1).

Fetching the ark was a good idea. What was not a good idea was transporting it on a cart rather than in the method prescribed by God, which was by poles run through the rings on the sides of the ark and carried on the shoulders of the Levites. You probably know what happened—the cart tipped, Uzzah reached out to steady the ark, and it cost him his life. A chastened David left the ark at Obed-Edom's place for three months and as a result, God blessed the household of Obed-Edom. Eventually, David regrouped for another try. This time he did it right, maybe even to the point of overkill; the text says that "when those who were carrying the ark of the LORD had taken six steps, [David] sacrificed a bull and a fattened calf" (2 Samuel 6:13). If that happened every six steps throughout the journey, then that means they would have had to sacrifice nearly three thousand bulls and three thousand calves along the way! Nice mess along the road.

A parallel account is found in 1 Chronicles, where we also discover a fascinating explanation by David of his original blunder: "It was because you, the Levites, did not bring it up the first time that the LORD our God broke out in anger against us. We did not inquire of him about how to do it in the prescribed way" (1 Chronicles 15:13). There's that word again: *inquire*. Like Joshua before him, David needed to learn that God is not satisfied with us making assumptions about the way He would like things done. The Lord likes to be asked.

David also learned that purity is crucial to God, even when it doesn't seem that vital. After all, wasn't the act of bringing the ark to Jerusalem much more important than the manner in which it was transported? Apparently not. So David penned this psalm. The first two verses are a prelude, focusing on God as Creator; the last four focus on the arrival of God as King of Glory at His sanctuary. The middle four verses focus on God as holy, specifying the qualifications one must possess to have access to Him:

> Who may ascend the hill of the LORD? Who may stand in his holy place? He who has clean hands and a pure heart, who does not lift up his soul to an idol or swear by what is false. He will receive blessing from the LORD and vindication from God his Savior. Such is the generation of those who seek him, who seek your face, O God of Jacob. Selah

> —Psalm 24:3-6

The qualifications of those who may "ascend" and "stand" in access to God are pretty stringent:
- "Clean hands"—purity of actions
- "Pure heart"—purity of attitudes and motives
- "Does not lift up his soul to an idol"—purity of worship
- "Or swear by what is false"—purity of truth-telling

That's a whole lot of purity! Psalm 15, which is quite similar thematically to the central portion of Psalm 24, adds a number of additional qualifications for those desiring to "dwell in [God's] sanctuary" and "live on [His] holy hill" (verses 2-3—blameless, righteous actions, no slander or wrongdoing, and so on). The entire "purity list" can be rather intimidating!

What is clear from these two psalms is that David served—and we serve—a holy God who determines our access to Him according to our purity. Back then, as now, it was pretty much impossible to attain, or maintain, that level of purity. It was (and is) the sacrifice of the high priest—in our case, Christ (Hebrews 7:27-28)—that provides the access to God through purity (1 John 1:7,9) that was (and is) unattainable otherwise. Yet God still expected purity in the life of David, and He still expects purity in our lives today if we are serious about upgrading our prayer lives:

> Dear friends, if our hearts do not condemn us, we have confidence before God and receive from him anything we ask, because we obey his commands and do what pleases him.
>
> —1 John 3:21-22

> You do not have, because you do not ask God. When you ask, you do not receive, because you ask with wrong motives, that you may spend what you get on your pleasures.
>
> —James 4:2-3

> Husbands, in the same way be considerate as you live with your wives, and treat them with respect as the weaker partner and as heirs with you of the gracious gift of life, so that nothing will hinder your prayers.
>
> —1 Peter 3:7

> The end of all things is near. Therefore be clear minded and self-controlled so that you can pray.
>
> —1 Peter 4:7

And when you stand praying, if you hold anything against anyone, forgive him, so that your Father in heaven may forgive you your sins.

—Mark 11:25

I am fully aware that I just took several pages to cover material that may be basic for many of us. We know, and teach our kids, that sin quenches the Spirit and hinders our prayer lives, and that confession of that sin restores the connection and access. But if we make a habit of watching R-rated movies in order to "better understand the culture," allowing the accompanying filth to infiltrate our minds and hearts, can we truly expect to be able to upgrade our prayer lives? Internet porn is a raging epidemic among pastors—including youth pastors. Our generation of youth workers needs to aspire to a new standard of purity. That alone will upgrade our prayer lives as much as anything.

I said earlier that I learned this the hard way. Amend that—I am *learning* this the hard way. Purity is a life-long struggle for most of us. Often, perhaps more often than not, the purity issue in our own hearts is not overt like Internet porn, but rather, more subtle. Yet ultimately, these more subtle "purity issues" are just as destructive if not checked.

For much of my Christian experience I have struggled with addictive behavior. The things that have entrapped me are for the most part not on the "list" of no-nos for Christians. These are things that you may do or partake of with no problem at all. But for me, it's Hebrews 12:1 "hindrance" stuff. That passage makes a distinction between "the sin that so easily entangles" and "everything that hinders"; the latter not being "sin-list" actions but a problem nonetheless. Both inhibit our ability to "run with perseverance the race marked out for us." And from time to time the Holy Spirit shows me something that is, for me, a hindrance. James 4:17 says, "Anyone, then, who knows the good he ought to do and doesn't do it, sins." It may not be sin for you but it has become so for me, and until I deal with it, my purity is compromised and, accordingly, so is my prayer life. When that happens, there is part of me that wants to respond like Evan Roberts to bring an outpouring of the Spirit. Roberts, a catalyst to the Welsh Revival in the early 1900s, penned these points that still apply to us today:

1. Is there any sin in your past that you have not confessed to God? On your knees at once. Your past must be put away, and yourself cleansed.
2. Is there anything in your life that is doubtful—anything that you cannot decide whether it is good or evil? Away with it. There must not be a cloud between you and God. Have your forgiven everybody, every, everybody? If not, don't expect forgiveness for your own sins. You won't get it.
3. Do what the Holy Spirit prompts you to do. Obedience—prompt, implicit, unquestioning obedience to the Spirit.
4. A public confession of Christ as your Savior. There is a vast difference between profession and confession.[2]

And there is a part of me that begins a lengthy season of justification and/or rationalization. For example, when I was an intern and seminary student my commute to class was nearly two hours, and often my first class was at 7:30 a.m. Several of us drove in a carpool two or three times a week. When it was my turn to drive, I needed help staying awake at the wheel. So I started drinking a brand of tea that had much more caffeine than coffee. Soon I began drinking tea on a daily basis; a local coffee house with a cool ambiance sold this spicy concoction that I loved. I'd often go there in the mornings to read the Word, journal, and study. I began meeting there with my discipleship groups. Yet after a while the Holy Spirit pointed out that I was addicted to the tea: "'Everything is permissible for me'—but not everything is beneficial. 'Everything is permissible for me'—but I will not be mastered by anything" (1 Corinthians 6:12). The ball was now in my court, and I struggled/justified/rationalized for far too long. It took the accountability of others (notably my wife) to help me gain freedom—and regain my purity—in this area.

I have been around more than a few world-class intercessors who need their cup of java to get going in the morning. It's not a problem for them, but it was for me. Coffee, tea, soft drinks, other "beverages," food in general, and numerous other items are permissible, but not if they master us. And the only way to really know is to ask the Holy Spirit. He will point out the negative influences in our lives, be it an entangling sin like Internet porn, or a hindrance like addiction to caffeine, talk radio, ESPN Sportscenter, or anything else that has the potential to distract us and compromise our purity. If you are really, truly desirous of an upgraded prayer life, right now might be a good time to ask Him: "Search me, O God, and know my heart; test me and know my anxious thoughts. *See if there is any offensive way in me*, and lead me in the way everlasting" (Psalm 139:23-24, emphasis added).

Besides just praying, being around people who pray, and removing all entanglements and hindrances to prayer, one of the better helps I have found for a prayer life upgrade is veteran prayer leader Dick Eastman's "10 Steps to a Practical, Joyful Prayer Life."[3] His steps (in italics), with some of my own comments added, are:

Find the best possible time and place for prayer. When we built our home, I designed a window seat for my office as my place of prayer. After a few years, I had to admit that my window seat fostered snoozing more than it did fervent prayer. The space heater I placed at my feet on cooler mornings was also a little too comfortable. I now have a prayer chair and use the space heater sparingly.

Forget all previous failures in prayer. Unless I did this, I would be prayer-paralyzed! My failures are legion, but so is my perseverance, so I seem to still be headed in the right direction.

Fight all prayer hindrances fiercely. The more alert we are, the better we can engage in this fight. Regrettably, it took years before I switched from my window seat to the chair. I also came to realize that the best way to deal with a wandering mind was to have a pen and paper handy; when a stray thought comes concerning my to-do list, I write it down, forget about it, and move on.

Focus on the Lord rather than on answers to prayer. The value of a relationship is not based on what the other person does for us, right?

Follow a meaningful plan of action. Sometimes prayer just "happens," but more often than not, it requires a workable plan, as opposed to an unrealistic plan. This might mean increasing the amount of time you set aside for prayer, or developing and maintaining a prayer list.

Feed every day on spiritual food. Our food is the Word of God. A practical way to make the transition from feeding on the Word to praying is to learn to make the prayers of the Bible our own prayers (many psalms and prayer passages in Paul's Epistles are good examples) by personalizing them.

Fellowship with the Lord in love. Prayer is a continual, developing relationship of mutual love and affection, not solely a duty of discipline.

Forgive every wrong done to you. If praying with what the Bible calls "clean hands and a pure heart" (Psalm 24:4) is Christianity 101, then this is Christianity 100.

Forsake all things that hinder spiritual growth, i.e. Evan Roberts' four points previously noted.

Finish what you start. Persistence is a key component in acts of prayer. When Jesus' disciples asked Him to teach them to pray, He gave them the model of what we call the Lord's Prayer, which was immediately followed by teaching on the importance of persistence.[4]

I could go on from here and discuss various methods of prayer—acronyms such as ACTS (Adoration, Confession, Thanksgiving, Supplication) or AWCIPA (Adoration, Waiting, Confession, Intercession, Petition, Adoration) are helpful to many. You may have come up with your own acronym or method that works for you. But whatever method(s) you decide to employ, your success in upgrading your prayer life will be determined to a large extent by the slogan popularized by shoe magnate Nike: "Just do it."[5]

Notes

1. I told you there would be a few "someone said's"!
2. Evan Roberts' four points to bring about an outpouring of the Spirit, see http://lifeaction.gospelcom. net/soro/settingthesails/content/delinterview.htm
3. Dick Eastman, "10 Steps to a Practical, Joyful, Prayer Life," *Pray!* Sept/Oct 2000, p. 14.
4. See Luke 11:1-13; the *NIV Study Bible* notes that the word for "boldness" in the text can also be translated "persistence."
5. I contend that Nike may have well lifted their slogan from Scripture: "His mother said to the servants, 'Whatever He says to you, do it'" (John 2:5, NASB).

6. COVERING YOUR REAR END[1]

The one concern of the devil is to keep Christians from praying. He fears nothing from prayerless studies, prayerless work and prayerless religion. He laughs at our toil, mocks at our wisdom, but trembles when we pray.

—Samuel Chadwick

How now does Satan hinder prayer? By temptation to postpone or curtail it by bringing in wandering thoughts and all sorts of distractions through unbelief and hopelessness.

—Andrew Murray

In 1986 my wife and I spent seven months doing youth ministry in Australia. Our time down under was, in Aussie slang, "fair dinkum!" (translation: really good). A decade later, I was asked to return to facilitate a four-day youth worker prayer summit and do some teaching on the role of united prayer in reaching cities for Christ. With great anticipation I boarded the plane for the long flight to Brisbane for a week, followed by another week in our "home" city of Melbourne. The good news was that ministry was tremendous; the not-so-good news was that I developed a killer case of jet-lag-induced insomnia. An hour or two of sleep per night for the first week was close to incapacitating. I finally tracked down an American coworker and was able to obtain some medicinal aids. Only then was I able get some snooze time before flying to Melbourne to facilitate the summit.

That summit was pretty powerful, so a year later I was invited back to Melbourne. This time, I literally couldn't sleep at all, and by the time day three of the summit arrived, I was a train wreck. During lunch, one of the summit participants who was also a doctor said to me, "Mike, you don't look too good. What's going on?" I explained my predicament and she whisked me away from our rural meeting site to a country doctor who could help me. That night, the Valium the doctor prescribed knocked me out for a good eight hours, and with the continued help of medication, I made it through the remainder of my stay.

But when I returned home and the Valium ran out, the sleeplessness persisted. For the next several months I subsisted on two or less hours of sleep a night, and I was in serious trouble—the wheels had come off and the chassis of my life was skidding down the racetrack to a grinding halt. Then, within the course of just a few days, three different intercessors from my fledgling prayer team, none of whom knew the others, contacted me because God had impressed upon them that I was the victim of some heavy-duty Australian witchcraft. I gathered my board at our home, they prayed appropriately, and my sleep patterns immediately made a radical shift toward normalcy.

This chapter is not about witchcraft, although that would be a lively and provocative discussion. Rather, this chapter is about spiritual protection—the kind we must provide for ourselves, our families, our ministries, and the kind we must solicit and receive from others. When I started out in youth ministry, spiritual warfare was a new, trendy, and controversial topic. That is not the case today. I am going to assume that you have at least a basic understanding that you and I, and the youth we work with, are targets, and the enemy of our souls is shooting some serious ammunition our way. It's no secret that today's young people are targets of demonic activity. One need not be particularly discerning to be aware of that fact. We understand the strategic nature of youth ministry, yet we are not alone in that understanding. The more kids Satan can distract, discourage, disillusion, depress, or derail, the better for him. And if he can do likewise to the leaders of those kids, the shepherds of God's flock, that's an even bigger coup. So if you didn't already realize it, welcome to the battle. Game on.

Dealing with witchcraft may not be a normal occurrence in your life or ministry, but let's realize that often the attacks of the enemy are more subtle, but just as destructive: the family argument that rises up when you're trying to get to church on Sunday morning (coincidence? I don't think so); the girl who shows up at your youth group dressed very provocatively and wants personal counseling; the email that directs you to a website that you know you shouldn't visit but think just one time wouldn't hurt anyone.[2] What I am saying is that no matter what the overt symptoms of attack may be, a passive approach to spiritual protection is an invitation to trouble.

The 2004 Summer Olympics, an American shooter had a gold medal pretty much wrapped up, but completely dropped out of medal contention on his last shot because he inexplicably aimed at, and hit, the wrong target. The enemy of our souls does not often hit the wrong target. The stakes are high, we are being targeted, and we had better be protected or we're going to get hit. Getting hit — I speak from too much personal experience — is not fun at all. So it is best to understand the nature of the battle, realize the covering of protection we have in Christ, and acknowledge that we are going to need help!

The Nature of the Battle

It is imperative for us to realize that the battle for the souls of young people is not merely "against flesh and blood, but against the rulers, against the authorities, against the powers of this dark world and against the spiritual forces of evil in the heavenly realms" (Ephesians 6:12). And as we engage in this battle, we are to be aware of demonic schemes "in order that Satan might not outwit us" (2 Corinthians 2:11).

On a corporate level, his strategy is to trash the church. The evidence that this strategy is working is obvious: local church struggles, factions, and splits; denominational battles; competition among organizations or within communities. On a personal level, his strategy is to trash us and our relationships with God, keeping us in spiritual darkness and bondage, and rendering us ineffective for kingdom work. He'll do that by temptation (Matthew 4:1-11; 1 Corinthians 7:5; 1 Thessalonians 3:5), false accusation (Revelations 12:10), physical affliction (2 Corinthians 12:7-10; Job), dividing relationships (Ephesians 4:25-27; 2 Corinthians 2:10-11), and a number of other means—including getting us to ignore the degree and subtlety of his influence (2 Corinthians 2:11), which makes the aforementioned strategies all the more effective!

The Covering of Christ

An additional strategy of the enemy is to introduce "FUD" into our hearts. Richard Wagner elaborates:

> In the marketing world, FUD is a term that refers to the practice of using disinformation as a weapon against your competitors. For example, a salesperson who is trying to make a sale against a rival company might employ FUD by stressing the inherent soundness and safety of her company's product versus the fear, uncertainty and doubt (FUD) that would ensue if one chose the competitor's product. In the same way, Satan runs his own disinformation campaign in a Christian's life by using fear, uncertainty, and doubt as a competitive weapon against God. He'd prefer that you trust the world's security instead of relying on God, and he'll use FUD to win.[3]

The enemy would like nothing more than to see fear immobilize or incapacitate us. He will also use fear to cause us to respond in our own strength. In my early, unmarried years of youth ministry, one of the many "interesting" places I lived was in the basement of a youth center our church had built in the downtown area of our city. One very late evening as I was preparing to climb up into bed (because my apartment's dimensions were a whopping eight by ten feet, I had hung my bed from the ceiling to give me more floor space), I clearly heard footsteps in the adjoining game room—a burglar! Being the mighty and fearless man of God that I was, I proceeded to wet my pants. Just kidding. I did, however, call 911, and for some strange reason, I also reacted by pulling my unloaded duck-hunting shotgun out of the closet, probably as some sort of double-barreled security blanket. The police soon arrived, and I went out the back door to greet them—with shotgun in hand. Bad move. The police shot me full of holes. Just kidding again. But as Ricky Ricardo would say, I had some "serious splainin' to do."[4]

Over my years of youth ministry, the enemy has made numerous attempts to "burglarize" my life, family, and ministry. FUD was often present in these early "power encounters," as were fleshly reactions and responses, which usually served to compound the problem. However, I have learned enough from my mistakes to now engage in spiritual battle—in the Spirit—with at least a measure of effectiveness. And a key in my ongoing transformation from wimp to warrior in God's army has been my understanding of the spiritual protection and covering I have in Christ. Bible teacher Lance Lambert writes:

> In these days when the Lord is calling the church around the world to battle stations, we need more than ever to understand our enemy. We also need to understand the rules of battle and how to fight from a place of complete safety and protection.[5]

Fear, along with uncertainty and doubt, is disabled in the stronghold of God. Spiritual protection is a theme that runs throughout the Bible. My personal favorite is Psalm 91 (take the time to check it out, perhaps even memorize it!) but there are many, many other relevant passages. Here are a few of them:

The LORD is a refuge for the oppressed, a stronghold in times of trouble. Those who know your name will trust in you, for you, LORD, have never forsaken those who seek you.

—Psalm 9:9-10

You are my hiding place; you will protect me from trouble and surround me with songs of deliverance.

—Psalm 32:7

God is our refuge and strength, an ever-present help in trouble. Therefore we will not fear, though the earth give way and the mountains fall into the heart of the sea, though its waters roar and foam and the mountains quake with their surging.

—Psalm 46:1-3

Every word of God is flawless; he is a shield to those who take refuge in him.

—Proverbs 30:5

But the Lord is faithful, and he will strengthen and protect you from the evil one.

—2 Thessalonians 3:3

Psalm 18 is very instructive in this regard as well, enough so that it warrants a closer look. Here, David asserts his confidence in God's protection:

I love you, O LORD, my strength. The LORD is my rock, my fortress and my deliverer; my God is my rock, in whom I take refuge. He is my shield and the horn of my salvation, my stronghold. I call to the LORD, who is worthy of praise, and I am saved from my enemies.

—vs. 1-3

David continues by describing an attack he experienced (vs. 4-5), his response of calling on the Lord for help (v. 6), God's awesome and powerful arrival on the scene (vs. 7-15), and God's rescue:

> He reached down from on high and took hold of me; he drew me out of deep waters. He rescued me from my powerful enemy, from my foes, who were too strong for me.
>
> —vs. 16-17

While Psalm 91 and the other aforementioned passages describe for us in vivid detail the protection we are afforded in the stronghold of God, in Psalm 18 David also delineates our responsibilities. Spiritual protection isn't a "given" to all Christians; there are responsibilities we must fulfill in order to gain access to God's stronghold:

> The Lord has dealt with me according to my righteousness; according to the cleanness of my hands he has rewarded me. For I have kept the ways of the Lord; I have not done evil by turning from my God. All his laws are before me; I have not turned away from his decrees. I have been blameless before him and have kept myself from sin. The Lord has rewarded me according to my righteousness, according to the cleanness of my hands in his sight.
>
> —vs. 20-24

What kept David protected? What keeps you and me safe within the stronghold of God? Holy living: confessing sin quickly and completely so we don't give the enemy a foothold (Ephesians 4:26-27), and living obediently. And when we are in that place, we not only have defensive protection, we have new offensive authority—we can "scale walls" (Psalm 18:29), bend bronze bows (v. 34), and our enemies will "turn their backs in flight" (v. 40)!

The Covering of Others

Paul understood the nature of the spiritual battle and our covering in Christ better than most, yet his writings are peppered with requests for prayer for protection:

> I urge you, brothers, by our Lord Jesus Christ and by the love of the Spirit, to join me in my struggle by praying to God for me. Pray that I may be rescued from the unbelievers in Judea and that my service in Jerusalem may be acceptable to the saints there.
>
> —Romans 15:30-31

> For I know that through your prayers and the help given by the Spirit of Jesus Christ, what has happened to me will turn out for my deliverance.
>
> —Philippians 1:19

> And pray that we may be delivered from wicked and evil men, for not everyone has faith.
>
> —2 Thessalonians 3:2

My personal favorite is 2 Corinthians 1:8-11:

> We do not want you to be uninformed, brothers, about the hardships we suffered in the province of Asia. We were under great pressure, far beyond our ability to endure, so that we despaired even of life. Indeed, in our hearts we felt the sentence of death. But this happened that we might not rely on ourselves but on God, who raises the dead. He has delivered us from such a deadly peril, and he will deliver us. On him we have set our hope that he will continue to deliver us, as you help us by your prayers. Then many will give thanks on our behalf for the gracious favor granted us in answer to the prayers of many.
>
> —2 Corinthians 1:8-11

Although Paul knew his protection ultimately had its source in Christ, he was also convinced that God would use the prayers of His people to help provide that protection. This is clear in the familiar Ephesians 6 passage concerning spiritual armor. Paul takes great pains to describe the various elements of our armor—the belt of truth, the breastplate of righteousness, the feet fitted with readiness from the gospel, the shield of faith, the helmet of salvation, the sword of the Spirit—all of which are afforded us as we abide in the stronghold of Christ. In fact, the armor is Christ Himself (see Romans 13:14). Yet Paul follows this with a description of the role of prayer in spiritual protection; it is poignant in that he is both instructive and personal here:

> And pray in the Spirit on all occasions with all kinds of prayers and requests. With this in mind, be alert and always keep on praying for all the saints. Pray also for me, that whenever I open my mouth, words may be given me so that I will fearlessly make known the mystery of the gospel, for which I am an ambassador in chains. Pray that I may declare it fearlessly, as I should.
> —Ephesians 6:18-20

While Scripture is not clear concerning the extent to which Paul had an organized team of prayer supporters, it is obvious that the covering provided by the intercession of others should be mandatory for those of us who are targeted by the enemy. C. Peter Wagner writes, "The most underutilized source of spiritual power in our churches today is intercession for Christian leaders."[6] We will be looking at ways of securing the covering of others through a prayer team in the next chapter.

Covering Your Family and Home

When I am away from home on a ministry assignment, my family sometimes gets a measure of spiritual harassment. There are seasons when it's more than sometimes. My wife will be awakened in the night with the sense that she is not alone; my son will struggle with nightmares; my daughter will try to cope with a variety of fears. To be sure, some of this is just life, but without question much of it is connected to what I do. And the attacks are not just confined to times when I am absent. I have spent many nighttime hours praying through our home, interceding for my family, and engaging in direct warfare. This is tough business; being a target is not fun, but it is preferable to having the devil target my home and family.

The experience of our family is not necessarily typical, but the enemy *will* try to infiltrate your home and family. Because he is a master of deceit and deception, the attacks will often be subtle or in the form of something that could be explained away, e.g. sicknesses, nightmares, arguments, temptations. As I have struggled through these types of attacks, I have learned two key principles that have brought a significant measure of victory in this area. First, I have been continually reminded that as the head of my household and family (see Ephesians 5:23-33 and 1 Timothy 2:11-14 concerning husbands; Ephesians 6:1-3 and Colossians 3:20 concerning children) I have the responsibility to help provide, through my prayers and spiritual leadership, protection and covering for my family.

Second, I have learned that if I will ask, the Lord will show me (or my wife, or my intercessors, or even on occasion my children) if a particular problem at home has its source in the wiles of the enemy or is simply a case of bad take-out Chinese food. Too often, we dismiss symptoms that *may* (emphasis here on "may") be indicative of spiritual harassment — chronic illness, including persistent nausea or headaches; recurrent bad dreams and nightmares; insomnia or unusual sleepiness; prolonged lack of peace; restless, disturbed, or even harassed children; a "heaviness" that lingers in your home — far too quickly. Part of that dismissal is a legitimate desire not to give the enemy too much credit. However, the danger of giving the devil too much credit is, in my mind, dwarfed by the danger of not recognizing his schemes. A spiritually protected home and family can be a wonderful place of refuge and rest, but we must realize that the enemy knows that, too, and will do all he can to disrupt it.

Living as a Target

Like it or not, youth ministry is spiritual warfare, and we who comprise God's army in this cosmic clash must learn to live as targets. So let's properly equip ourselves to do battle against the spiritual forces of darkness that take aim at us, and make sure that as we contend in battle for the lives of the emerging generations of young people, we are doing so with the support of others who are committed to interceding on our behalf. And let's also recognize that this kind of prayer support is not only important for us and our families, it is also imperative for our ministries, as will be discussed in the next chapter.

Notes

1. Much of the content of this chapter is adapted from chapters 7 and 8 of my book, *Youth Ministry from the Inside Out* (Downers Grove, Ill.: InterVarsity, 2003). In my opinion, it is important enough that it bears repeating here.
2. Space does not allow for a lengthy discussion of this issue, although involvement in Internet porn is a runaway freight train among those in ministry, if the researchers are at all accurate. There are a number of helpful tools available — filters, accountability software, and so on — that should be standard issue to all youth workers.
3. Richard Wagner, *Christian Prayer for Dummies* (New York: Wiley Publishing, 2003), p. 171.
4. It turns out there *was* a burglar in the youth center, but he escaped out a window before the police arrived.
5. Lance Lambert, *Spiritual Protection* (Tonbridge, Kent, England: Sovereign World Limited, 1991), p. 5.
6. C. Peter Wagner, *Prayer Shield* (Ventura, Calif: Regal Books, 1992), p. 19.

PART III: THE PRAYING YOUTH MINISTRY

7. THE PRAYER-DRIVEN YOUTH MINISTRY

Prayer is the ministry, and the ministry is prayer.

—Unknown

As it is the business of tailors to make clothes and of cobblers to mend shoes, so it is the business of Christians to pray.

—Martin Luther

I hadn't been a Christian very long when I entered vocational youth ministry, so I hadn't had time to forget some of the basic tenets of the faith that I was taught—and experienced—as a new believer. One of those tenets concerned prayer: "No prayer, no power; some prayer, some power; much prayer, much power!" I think that's reasonable theology. I did back then as well. Perhaps my motives were a bit more mixed than they are now ("No prayer, no success; some prayer, some success; much prayer, much success and fame!"). Regardless, I wanted to make sure our youth ministry involved much prayer. So I scheduled a regular prayer time for our volunteer team—Monday through Friday from 6:30 to 7:15 a.m.

I know, I was naïve and idealistic, but for a year and a half I only missed two gatherings, and I almost always had "two or more gathered" with me—usually four to eight, and sometimes many more.

Let me be quick to add the necessary caveats. I was serving in a college town, so most of the volunteers were students who lived within a few minutes of our place of prayer and many had to get up that early for classes anyway. That level of commitment probably wouldn't (and didn't) work in other locales, but for our season, we prayed up a storm. Our venue was a building we were praying into service—an old American Legion hall that would soon become a church-run community youth center. For most of our season of prayer, we had one bare bulb for light and a space heater to huddle around in the cold of winter. We also had a journal in which we recorded our prayers and their answers. I still have the journal. One doesn't easily dispose of such an amazing record of God's faithfulness.

During that season of youthful exuberance, the prayer/power principle was embedded in my ministry DNA. But it wasn't until years later that I came to realize what I mentioned last chapter, that "much prayer" means not only much prayer on the part of me and my team, but it also means much prayer from a group of folks who are committed to supporting me and my ministry on a consistent basis. So, I went about developing a ministry prayer team.

Prayer Team Particulars

There are, I have discovered through trial and much error, a variety of ways to go about this. Rather than give you a particular model to follow, I would like to give you some principles that I have gleaned, both from others (notably C. Peter Wagner, who writes extensively on this subject in his book, *Prayer Shield*) and from my own experiences with prayer teams, that should be of some help to you as you develop your own working model. (And I'm trusting that the previous chapter helped you to see how important this is!)

Prayer team members should be intentionally recruited. There are at least two strategies in this regard: issuing a broad call for prayer support to your congregation, friends, and supporters, and hand-picking those you think might have an interest and asking them personally. I have used a combination of both methods. Because I now lead a nonprofit organization, I started my recruiting by describing my need in my monthly newsletter and asking people to respond if they had an interest. To those who responded, I gave more details about what they were getting themselves into. If they felt the Lord leading them, they would join the team. Then, as time passed and I sensed the need for a deeper level of personal prayer support, I recruited a select group of people by personal invitation. Back when I was a local church youth pastor, I issued a broad call to our congregation for prayer support for our ministry. I took the initiative to issue special invitations to senior citizens (many of whom love to pray for kids) and parents, and when I discovered who the intercessors were in the church, I heartily went after them. All of it was, and is, intentional. I know of many youth workers who consistently ask their congregations to pray for them and their ministries. While that is commendable, it is not a substitute for the intentional development of a prayer team.

Quality is more important than quantity. A case can be made for "the more, the merrier" idea when it comes to prayer supporters. Peter Wagner has hundreds on his team, and the founder of Campus Crusade for Christ, the late Bill Bright, estimated his team to number in the thousands. My prayer team currently numbers around seventy-five. Yet, I have found that when my team grows to three figures, I lose some of the personal connection that, for me, is an important component of my prayer support. And when I was a local church youth pastor, my prayer supporters usually numbered less than a dozen, and that size worked great! Which do you think is more effective—a hundred folks who pray for you on an occasional basis, or a dozen who pray consistently, even daily, and take the initiative to stay current concerning your personal and ministry prayer needs?

There can be different levels of your prayer team, depending on your degree of involvement in ministry and your inquiring of the Lord. Wagner's support consists of three levels of prayer supporters,[1] while I have two levels on my team. The point is not the number of levels, but rather, the reason for different levels. What I call Level One are folks who have committed to pray for my ministry, my family, and me on a relatively consistent basis. They may not know all the details concerning my prayer needs or those of my family and ministry, or myself, but they pray, and I need them desperately. Level Two comprises a dozen people who feel called to intercede for me. In most cases, I have recruited them. These folks often need more information, so I communicate with them more regularly and in greater detail. I also let them know that when they hear anything from the Lord about me or my ministry, I want to hear it, too!

Communication is the key to your prayer team. I emphasized in chapter 3 the importance of two-way communication in your personal prayer life. The same principle holds true here, as it does in any kind of relationship. I use email to communicate with the two levels of my prayer team. I also send quarterly mailings to those pray-ers who don't use email. No matter what my means of communication, I try to keep it simple. To be honest, when I receive a prayer letter with a lengthy list of requests, I usually don't cover them all. So, in my own communication, I try to identify several specific areas in my ministry and family life. Pray-ers who request additional information receive it. And I remind them to tell me what the Lord is saying to them about my family, my ministry, and me. In some circles, this is called a prophetic word, or "word" for short. Regardless of what it is called, I think most of us would agree that God does, indeed, speak to us today through other people. When three of my intercessors told me I had been attacked spiritually in Australia, I trusted them. God confirmed their discernment in my own spirit as well, and it resulted in a major breakthrough. I received prophetic words from several sources concerning the sabbatical I took while writing this book, and concerning the actual writing project itself. I do not take these "words" lightly. Experience has shown me that time and time again, God has spoken in significant and strategic ways through my intercessors.

Involvement on your prayer team is not a lifelong commitment. It is a good idea to give folks an "out" should they no longer be able, or willing, to meet the commitments as a prayer team member. Don't assume that they will let you know if they want off; they usually won't—they'll just quit praying. Express your gratitude for their prayer support, and release them with your blessing!

A prayer team is not the same as a support team. Those of us who have the privilege of raising personal financial support need to make a clear distinction between our prayer supporters and our financial supporters. Often folks do both for us, but it is unwise to assume that financial supporters are always also prayer supporters (or vice versa).

Beyond the Prayer Team

A buddy of mine who is a missionary-turned-trucker has had some recent insider exposure, through his deliveries, to a rather large chain of retail stores. He has some interesting stories to tell about the "culture" of this market monster. Some of the stories are pretty funny, but through them it's apparent that one of the reasons this particular chain is successful is that they have created a "culture of success." True, they have a house newsletter full of pithy corporate sayings, and rumor has it that each store starts off the day with some group singing, but the culture of success among employees—from the CEO to the janitor—is pervasive, and their bottom line boasts gargantuan profits.

An effective prayer-driven youth ministry is one that is successful at creating a "culture of prayer" both within and surrounding the ministry, so that participation in prayer becomes similarly pervasive. This happens when, among other things:

- The leader becomes a raging, foaming-at-the-mouth champion of prayer. And that can be you! (Maybe it already is.)
- Prayer infuses *everything* to the extent that the ministry is known as a praying ministry, just as the leader is known as a praying leader.

- A designated prayer team is in place and functioning.
- Ample opportunities are provided for everyone and anyone to participate in ministry-related prayer initiatives.
- Students are mentored and mobilized in the area of prayer (more detail on this in the next chapter).
- Students are the recipients of consistent, persistent, prevailing prayer.

The first five of these have been covered, or will be covered, in more depth. But let's focus for a minute on the last one. As youth leaders, one of our primary responsibilities is the shepherding and discipling of young people. If you are a vocational youth worker, this is likely at the top of your job description. If you are a volunteer, if this isn't at or near the top of your ministry description, it should be. My experience is that the amount of time and energy youth workers spend praying for kids is not commensurate to the time they spend with them at youth group or church, in small groups, in Sunday school discussions, or even over a mocha latte at Starbucks. It bears repeating, and emphasizing, that the most effective youth work is relational and incarnational. It also bears mentioning that *the most effective transformational* youth work takes place in the arena of prayer.

Though we may already know this, chances are we don't put it into practice as we should. When Samuel committed to discipling the Israelites in "the way that is good and right," he prefaced that commitment with another: "As for me, far be it from me that I should sin against the LORD by failing to pray for you" (1 Samuel 12:23). Prayer was, for him, the most significant way in which he could influence his people.

Paul's prayer commitment to his closest disciple, Timothy, was to the extent that "night and day I constantly remember you in my prayers" (2 Timothy 1:3). And many of Paul's letters to city churches and regional groups of churches are peppered with commitments to pray for them, as well as actual written prayers (see 2 Corinthians 13:9; Ephesians 1:15-23;

3:14-19; Philippians 1:3-11; Colossians 1:3,9-12; 1 Thessalonians 1:2-3; 2 Thessalonians 1:11-12; Philemon 1:4-6). There's one more example—Jesus. How many of us have literally stayed up all night praying about the students we would ask to be on our leadership team or in our small group (Luke 6:12-16)? It's legitimate to assume that at least part of Jesus' frequent solitary prayer times (Matthew 14:23; Mark 1:35; Luke 5:16) was devoted to prayer for His disciples and apostles.

Effective intercession for students is both *biblical* and *practical*. I have included in the appendix a list of thirty-one biblical ways to pray for youth, along with the corresponding Scripture references. You can probably discover additional biblical prayers yourself. These kinds of prayers should be supplemented by practical prayers for the issues and needs of students. Obviously, we need to know what those issues are in order to emphasize the relational aspect of youth work. There have been times when I have called through my list of students with no other purpose than to ask them how I can pray for them, often praying right then and there over the phone. When they realize that the purpose of my call is not the "standard" one—to ask why they weren't at the latest youth activity, or to remind them to register for the retreat—students are usually pleasantly surprised and encouraged. The same holds true when the caller is not a youth pastor or youth worker, but a member of your prayer team. Be sure to consistently feed your prayer team biblical and practical resources to fuel their praying!

A Few More Ideas for Prayer-Driven Ministries
One of the main thrusts of this book is to help the development of prayer-driven youth ministries as well as prayer-driven youth *ministers*.[2] As you read through the chapters to come you will see numerous practical prayer ideas and suggestions, which will help you create a culture of prayer. In addition, I would like to give you a short list of ideas that don't seem to fit well elsewhere, but are helpful in prayer culture development.

Prayer Flash Cards — Taking digital photos of students and recording relevant information about each student helps me to keep track of them and their prayer needs and requests. I used to do this with photo prints, but with the arrival of the digital age, the photos migrated to my laptop database along with the regularly updated prayer requests.

Website Prayer Page — Websites that are typically full of calendars, photos, blogs, and the like can be greatly enhanced with a prayer page. The capability of receiving prayer requests from students, staff, parents, and others, on a prayer page will make it even better.

Prayer Resources — A student-friendly prayer resource library, which can be combined with online resources, can both stimulate those in your sphere of influence concerning prayer and provide the tools that those who are already "stimulated" might need. The website for our youth ministry movement in Portland is full of resources in Portable Document Format (PDF) that students can download and use. A number of local church-based youth ministry sites I have visited as of late have similar resources.

Custom-Designed Prayer Journals — There are a number of excellent prayer journals on the market. Customizing them helps make them more personal for youth. Getting a team of young people involved in this journal development process generates ownership and helps create a product that is by youth, for youth, and usable by youth.

On a physical level, you and I are pretty much stuck with our DNA. Yet on a spiritual level, we can undergo spiritual "gene therapy" that can make us raging, foaming-at-the-mouth prayer champions. When that happens, when we surround ourselves with a prayer team of folks with prayer genes, and when we come to expect prayer to be an essential component of every dimension of our ministries, then we have developed prayer-driven youth ministries. And then we have set the stage for some very cool stuff to happen—that is, after we have given prayer gene therapy to our students.

Notes

1. See Wagner's *Prayer Shield* for the details of his personal prayer teams.
2. The phrase "prayer-driven youth ministry" is by no means implying any superiority to the "purpose-driven youth ministry" philosophy so capably espoused by Doug Fields in the book by the same title, and championed on a personal and church-wide level by Rick Warren at Saddleback Community Church.

8. MENTORING AND MOBILIZING STUDENTS IN PRAYER

The men upon whose shoulders rested the initial responsibility of Christianizing the world came to Jesus with one supreme request. They did not say, "Lord, teach us to preach," "Lord, teach us to do miracles," or "Lord, teach us to be wise" . . . but they said, "Lord, teach us to pray."

—Billy Graham

Beginning high in the Cascade Mountain Range of central Oregon, the Deschutes River meanders south through alpine meadows before making a sweeping turn north and cutting a deep canyon through the high desert of my home state, eventually joining the Columbia River and heading west to the ocean. Extremely popular with white-water rafting enthusiasts, the canyon is also famous for the "railroad wars" of the late 1800s, when rival railroad barons raced on opposing sides of the river to complete rail lines up the canyon. The tycoon on the west side won, and the roar of freight trains rolling down the tracks punctuates a present-day experience on the paradoxically dangerous yet calming waters of the Deschutes. One of the more popular rapids is known as "Boxcar," marking the location where a runaway freight train jumped the tracks and deposited a few cars in the river.

The Deschutes is also a blue-ribbon trout stream, home of large and elusive "Deschutes Redside" rainbow trout. I go there as often as I can for emotional and spiritual therapy, throwing artificial flies at wary trout while stumbling on slippery rocks and filling my waders with the cool water. On occasion, a trout with a lower IQ will inhale my offering, and the fight begins. Because of the swiftness of the current and the size of the resident fish, there are times when a hooked trout will head downstream with reckless abandon. There is no stopping it! One can only hold on to the rod and hope that the trout tires and retreats before the line snaps. My buddies and I call this experience getting "freight-trained."

There is a rapidly growing number of youth who are fast becoming a runaway freight train within the prayer movement. They are represented by the millions who participate in See You at the Pole, praying around their school flagpoles the third Wednesday in September each year, and by the hundreds of thousands who have attended The Call in Washington, D.C., Pasadena, San Francisco, Dallas, and other cities for twelve hours of fasting and intense corporate prayer. They are the ones who engage in "thirty-second kneel downs" in front of their lockers as they intercede for their schools and classmates, and gather in concerts of prayer to worship and pray with passion.

As youth workers, we are the shepherds of this emerging generation. We are in essence the conductors of this "runaway freight train" of praying youth. As such, we have a solemn responsibility to keep them on track, so to speak: to harness their passion without quenching it; to give them direction without lording it over them; to mentor them in prayer with humility, acknowledging that in many cases, *they* may be the ones who are mentoring *us*. And, we are called to increase their tribe.

That being said, for every student who is a praying freight-trainer, there are a handful that are not even aware that there is a train! But my experience is that the transition from neophyte to praying freight-trainer is not necessarily a lengthy one for students. So, put on your conductor's cap and join me in a crash course entitled, "The Dynamics of a Runaway

Freight Train." Our course will consist of three topics: Conducting Basics (becoming a prayer leader), Configuring the Cars on the Train (mentoring and mobilizing students in prayer), and Proper Operation of the Bellows (fanning the fires of passion without extinguishing them or allowing them to explode out of control).

Conducting Basics

During my sixteen-year tenure as a local church youth pastor, prayer was a critical component of my ministry philosophy. Hindsight is usually 20/20, and from today's perspective I would characterize my prayer mentoring and mobilization efforts back then as elementary at best. But at the time, we were doing what we thought was some good work.

Our volunteer team of youth workers was well schooled in spiritual warfare and intercessory prayer. Students were mobilized to pray for their schools and peers in creative ways. A prayer team supported our ministry. Yet my honest assessment would be that, at best, only 15 to 20 percent of our students were of "freight train" quality in the area of prayer. The rest could be characterized as lukewarm, indifferent, or ignorant concerning personal or corporate prayer. They had little passion for prayer, had not experienced the power of prayer, and certainly were not well-heeled in the practice of prayer.

My experience in the ensuing years leads me to believe that most youth ministries consist of similar percentages. The minority is passionate about prayer, and the majority falls into other categories. Some youth workers have a significant number of students who qualify as "freight-trainers" in prayer. Others have few, or maybe even none, who are excited about and engaged in prevailing prayer.

This need not be the case. It may not be realistic to have a youth ministry full of praying freight-trainers (although I'd rather be idealistic than realistic), but we can help *all* of our students grow in prayer—and who knows how many "freight-trainers" may emerge from our ministries. We do not start by making sure that our youth ministry philosophy includes "building a prayer base," as important as that is. We start with ourselves.

Several chapters ago I mentioned that prayer, as with any spiritual discipline, is as much "caught" as "taught." We must have a personal *passion* about prayer. We must have a *plan* to see that passion imparted to our students. We must *persevere* in the implementation of that passion. Our *passion* for prayer must be grown out of our passion for Jesus, but it must also be apparent to our students that we are seriously "into" prayer. Passion and enthusiasm are imparted or "caught" much more easily than they are "taught"; you need both, but the former will give power to the latter. Our *plan* must be based on seeking the Lord and inquiring of Him concerning His purposes for our ministries regarding prayer. As I mentioned earlier, if that is not the case, our plan will become program-based and will not endure. And our *perseverance* must be born out of the strength of our passion and our convictions concerning His plan. Kids will be kids, and there will be seasons in all of our ministries when they seem to not care about prayer or praying, and even the freight-trainers will seem to be stuck on the tracks.

Configuring the Cars on the Train

In the next few pages you are *not* going to get the latest, greatest program for turning your students into prayer freight-trainers. What you *will* get are resources for your prayer tool-box, or at least some direction as to where to go to get the tools. Tools in a toolbox are only as effective as the skillfulness of the one using them. If you are led to make use of some of them (ask the Holy Spirit to show you which tools are for *your* kids and *your* ministry), be sure that you are personally practicing them as well. All won't work for you. Some simply won't connect with your kids. Others may not be appropriate for your church situation. (In other words, ask *before* you construct a prayer labyrinth in your church fellowship hall.) Additionally, you likely have some of your own prayer tools, not included here, practices you have found to be guaranteed "home runs" with kids.

Mentoring Basics

Allow me to preface what is below with a caveat: *mentoring* is a trendy word today, and while its use is valuable, a more preferable word as far as I'm concerned is *discipling*. It's biblical, it connotes the impartation of spiritual truths and principles for living, and it sets itself apart from secular mentoring. So, while I will use *mentoring* here, feel free to substitute *discipling*.

Lee Brase served as the prayer ministry coordinator for The Navigators for many years and has mentored many people, young and old, in prayer. He offers five suggestions in the area of mentoring others:

1. *Use Scripture.* I have been privileged to have been asked by many people to mentor them in prayer. The most effective way I have found to do this is to take them to the prayers in the Bible. I believe that God has recorded prayers in Scripture for every occasion: for praise, thanks, times of grief, pain, frustration, warfare, joy, inner needs, and more.
2. *It's extremely difficult — but necessary — for people to "unlearn" bad prayer habits* — praying about surface issues rather than the underlying issues; lengthy, wordy prayer rather than simply getting to the point; prayers that are directed to the people in the room rather than to God; prayers that focus primarily on asking rather than devotion and praise; praying from our perspective rather than seeking to pray from God's perspective.
3. Prayer works because of the volume of faith — not the volume of prayer.
4. Praying people and the prayers of the Bible should be our mentors.
5. Asking is the easy part of prayer; knowing what to ask is the difficult part.[1]

Veteran intercessor Candy Abbott provides some additional tips on mentoring:
- Pray often with and for the person whom you are mentoring.

- In prayer situations, encourage your student to *increase* while you *decrease*. That is, resist the urge to take over. Let him do whatever he is willing and able to do.
- Be patient. Lead, but do not push. Let the student progress at the prompting of the Holy Spirit.
- Be prepared to make an investment in time and emotion. Be aware that, as a bond of trust develops, your pupil will open up to you and share her innermost feelings.[2]

In my own mentoring experiences, I have found two common fears among students:
- Fear of praying out loud. Many students (and adults) are intimidated by this. The reasons are varied, the most prominent being lack of confidence. It's helpful here to encourage them gradually. A good place to start is to give them a sentence prayer to finish, such as "I praise You, God, because You are . . . ." Or, "Thank you, Lord, for . . . ." Encourage their successes. Remind them that God is more concerned about the attitude of the heart than the adequacy of vocabulary. Don't place students in a position where they have to pray out loud in a group setting unless you know they have some measure of experience and/or comfort in doing so. The resulting embarrassment for them is counterproductive to prayer mentoring. Encourage them to pray out loud during their own devotional times (tell them that will also help them stay focused in their praying). Be sure they hear you pray out loud for them.
- Fear of not knowing what to pray. Make your instructions concerning prayer as specific as possible. I have also found it helpful to give students prayer models— specifically targeted prayers that are written down. Students can pray them as their own, and will eventually be able to modify them to make them more personal. (See the appendix for some examples of model prayers.)

Prayer Tools (Helps)

There are countless prayer tools out there. We must take the time to look for them and ask the Lord for direction concerning which ones are appropriate for our ministries and our students. Until recently, there hasn't been much published in the youth ministry realm concerning prayer. But that is changing—there are books currently on the market that consist almost entirely of prayer helps and tools.[3] To whet your appetite, here are a few examples of tools I have found helpful:

Acronyms—These are a great way to help kids learn how to pray. One of the most popular acronyms for a prayer method is ACTS—Adoration, Confession, Thanksgiving, and Supplication. Another is PRAY—Praise, Repent, Ask, Yield. Create your own if you prefer.

Prayer Lists and Journals—Many use these, but few use them well. I have found that the more elaborately structured the lists and/or journals are, the more difficult it is for youth to use them consistently over the long run. The purpose of a prayer list is to write prayer requests so you can pray for them in an orderly and consistent manner while recording God's faithfulness in answering prayer. A prayer journal can have room for a prayer list and also provide space for students to write out their prayers—many find this beneficial because it helps them stay focused. Try to find one that has a short learning curve (is easy to follow), or custom-make your own lists and journals for your students.

Prayer and Worship/Prayer Retreats—My friend Wayne attended a youth worker prayer summit I facilitated, and now he was on the phone, wanting me to fly across the country to lead a similar event for his youth group. We would start on Friday night, finish with lunch on Sunday, and our agenda would consist of prayer. That was it—no mixers, no speakers, and no wild outdoor games. The kids knew they were signing up for a prayer retreat, but they had no clue how literally that would be taken. I took the assignment with a bit of trepidation, which was validated when we arrived at the venue and Wayne briefed his students. There were a lot of big eyes and open mouths. "We're going to do *what*?"

But guess what? We made it. Kids who had never prayed continuously for more than a half hour were completely "stoked" that they had prayed in a number of creative ways — and worshiped, because it's often hard to separate the two — *for an entire weekend*. The point is that youth can do this. And it will have a bigger impact on their lives than a low-est-common-denominator "Kumbaya Klub" retreat ever could.

Campus Prayer Tools — See chapter 10, "Prayer for the Campus, Community, and City," for a wide variety of tools in this area.

Other Contemplative Tools — Sacred reading, silence and solitude, meditation, and centering prayer are among the many prayer forms practiced by Catholics, orthodox believers, and many mainline denominational believers for centuries. The broader church is rediscovering the value of these practices. Prayer labyrinths are showing up at youth conferences. Prayer icons are appearing on the walls of youth rooms. The Jesus Prayer and centering prayer are starting to infiltrate evangelical circles. This is a very good thing! Many of these practices may be new to you, so take the time to find out what they are all about. It will be worth it to your kids and to you as well. Be aware that because of the historical ties of many of these prayers, some of you may need to be prepared for a little criticism or opposition to their use.

One additional thing to remember when using these or any other prayer tool is that widely-accepted educational theory asserts that the more "gates" (the sensory portals of hearing, seeing, speaking, touching, and smelling[4]) you can use to impart information, the better it will be received and utilized. Think: Students *hearing* you and others pray and *seeing* others pray communicates that it's "legit" to pray or be in the presence of praying people—even with your eyes open! Often the facial and/or body expressions of praying people are quite instructive: bowed heads or uplifted hands or bended knees. And students can speak aloud their own prayers, hold the Scriptures or a prayer book in their hands as they pray, or, if they are Catholic, handle a rosary. Smelling incense in a place of prayer can stimulate pray-ers.

Proper Operation of the Bellows

Once upon a time, God showed up at one of my summer camps. His Presence was palpable and it shook us all. We worshiped and prayed for hours. Almost everyone there who was not saved got saved, and we were up most of the night unable to sleep. Many of those kids returned home changed. For some, the change was short-lived, but the cause of that was, at least in part, a "fan failure" on my part. Paul exhorts Timothy to "fan into flame the gift of God" (2 Timothy 1:6). When I had a bunch of kids who were ready for some serious fanning, I wasn't sure how to do that. (I hadn't read this book yet!)

When our kids look as if they might become prayer freight-trainers—a result of a unique experience, mentoring, or maybe God firing them up through some other reason—we need to encourage them as best we can, playing our part, as shepherds, in the "fanning" process. All of our students need to get a periodic "fanning" when it comes to prayer, but when we identify those who are F.A.T. (Faithful, Available, and Teachable), they warrant more focused attention. That is true mentoring/discipling; Jesus "fanned" His disciples with a gentle breeze, used a stronger wind with His apostles, and let loose the hurricane on Peter, James, and John. Who knows, perhaps some of the kids in our groups today will be the George Müller, Rees Howell, Evelyn Christenson, or Bobbie Byerly of tomorrow!

Notes

1. Lee Brase, "The Word on Mentoring," *Pray!*, Mar/Apr 2000, pp. 14-17.
2. Candy Abbott, "Tips on Mentoring," *Pray!*, Mar/Apr 2000, p. 20.
3. Three examples of good youth ministry resources in the area of prayer are *Soul Shaper* by Tony Jones (Grand Rapids, Mich. Youth Specialties, 2003), *The Book of Uncommon Prayer* by Steven L. Case (El Cajon: Calif. Youth Specialties, 2002), and *Transforming Prayers: 40 Unique Experiences for Youth* by Jenny Baker (Loveland, Colo.: Group Publishing, 2003).
4. You might wonder about smelling, but incense is once again gaining popularity as a prayer aid.

9. TACTICS FOR BIG EVENTS

When we work, we work. When we pray, God works.

—J. Hudson Taylor

I was way over my head and I knew it. Sure, I had organized prayer support for some of our youth group's outreaches, and I had led small teams of intercessors in prayer during the evangelistic youth rallies that accompanied the Billy Graham Crusade held in my hometown of Portland, Oregon, in 1992. But this was taking prayer support to a whole new level—ten entire days of on-site prayer coverage for twenty-five thousand students attending Youth for Christ's two DC/LA '94 Youth Evangelism Super Conferences in Washington, D.C., and Los Angeles, California. I knew I needed help . . . and fast!

It all started innocently enough. I was teaching at a YFC regional conference on the importance of prayer in youth ministry. One conversation led to another, and before I knew it, I was committed to mobilizing and deploying on-site prayer support for two gigantic youth events. So I started making calls for help.

Chuck Pierce is a name familiar to many as one of the leaders of the global prayer movement and a prolific author on a variety of prayer-related subjects. Back then, Chuck was an emerging leader, so to speak, and he agreed to join me in D.C. to teach me the ropes of on-site prayer. Chuck was the point person for our team of about a dozen folks from all over the United States. For the most part I played the role of human sponge again, soaking in everything I could. We arrived the day before the conference began. Under Chuck's leadership we engaged in a prayerwalk of the conference venue, in spiritual warfare in the convention hall where the general sessions were to be held, and in worship and intercession in the prayer room to which we were assigned.

Once the students arrived, we continued in the same pattern for about ten hours a day. I continued to play the part of associate leader/human sponge until day three, when Chuck informed me that he had another commitment in the D.C. area and I would be leading our prayer team that morning. With much trepidation I sent a few from our team to pray in various venues and stayed with a group of about ten in our prayer room. Things seemed to be going well until the entire group started praying in their "prayer languages." They prayed loudly. At the same time. And for a very long time. And so, being the strong, discerning leader I was, I quit and went home. Well, not really, but at the time I sure wished Chuck were there!

Since then, I have led on-site prayer teams for nearly a dozen big events—a half-dozen DC/LA conferences, the Atlanta '96 Youth Worker Conference, and a variety of other local and regional gatherings. And my experience in D.C. in '94 was just the tip of the iceberg when it comes to, shall we say, *different* experiences with prayer teams. At one venue, a team member stood at the window of our prayer room that overlooked the auditorium and started honking loudly. When I asked him what he was doing, he replied that he had the gifting of being a *shofar* (a ram's horn frequently used in the Old Testament for either a call to worship or a call to battle) and was exercising his gift. In another venue, we had a mutiny of sorts on our prayer team. A few of the members felt we needed to proceed in an entirely different direction from our present course, and eventually left to go their own way in a different room. (Now *that* gave the conference leadership a lot of confidence in what we were doing!)

I've got numerous war stories—some humorous, some definitely not so. But for every unusual story, I have *many* more memories of God working in and through our on-site teams in ways that significantly enhanced the spiritual impact of the events. In DC/LA '94, twenty thousand students were gathering at the Capitol Mall for a culminating rally and the weather report was not good. Thunderstorms were forecast for the area, and they could be seen approaching the Mall as we gathered there. Canceling the rally was a serious possibility, given the imminent danger of lightning strikes. Standing behind the stage, our team was briefed by the DC/LA leadership.

Then Chuck deployed us: some prayerwalking the venue; others standing in a corner, hands raised against the approaching thunderheads, agreeing in prayer that God would move the storm. In a clearly supernatural experience, the approaching clouds did a 180-degree turn, headed the other way, and the rally continued! This caught the attention of the DC/LA leadership in a profound way and was the seminal event in transforming DC/LA prayer support from an experiment to an integral part of their ongoing strategy.

Stories like this may fit into the category of "really cool." But the many incidents of the prayer team being led in a particular direction in our prayer room, and then seeing what we had prayed about "in secret" being birthed out in the arena among the students, fall into the "really, really cool" category for sure. The unity of folks from around the country who didn't know each other very well coming together to pray God's desires into reality was nothing short of amazing. It's those stories that authenticate and validate the importance of prayer support for strategic "Big Events."

Why Focus on Big Events?

Most of us are aware that the optimal context for spiritual change is relationships. As youth workers, the greatest long-term impact we will have with students is in the context of being both relational and incarnational. We must be "with" students in their world and allow the transfer of applicable truth to take place in that context. However, the big events of our ministries—retreats, camps, conferences, rallies, crusades, missions trips—are often "booster rockets" that propel a student far ahead in his or her spiritual pilgrimage in a short period of time. Major personal decisions are often made at big events, whether they are decisions to follow Christ, commitments to personal holiness, decisions to stay sexually pure, commitments to personal evangelism, or the choices to pursue careers in ministry or missions. Although these decisions must be verified and solidified in the context of relationships, discipleship, and daily living, they are nevertheless vital and often life-changing decisions. As youth workers we must do all we can to make these big events as significant and life changing as possible. And what better way to accomplish that than through prayer?

The goal of any big-event prayer strategy is to create an environment, through prayer, that will produce maximum spiritual impact in the lives of a maximum number of students in a minimum amount of time. Certainly prayer for the more tangible elements of big events—the location, cost, program, speaker, worship, music, activities—is very important. Creating or attending a poorly staged big event that does not capture the imagination or attention of students presents an obstacle when it comes to creating an environment for spiritual impact through prayer. On the other hand, a high-quality event with all the bells and whistles but little or no prayer strategy is no better. I have seen mediocre events in terms of structure and content, but because they were bathed in concerted prayer, they had a dynamic spiritual impact on students. And I have seen events that featured high profile speakers and musicians, a multitude of audiovisual delights, and enough fog machines to shut down an airport, yet the impact on students' lives was minimal because prayer was sacrificed on the altar of programming.

Big events differ greatly in their purpose and content, and prayer strategy particulars can differ greatly from venue to venue. However, the governing principles that determine the strategy remain relatively constant. This chapter will address the scenario of a youth leader preparing to bring his or her students to a big event (such as DC/LA) that is staged by someone else, although the principles are certainly applicable to a self-staged big event. For you and your ministry, that may be a dozen kids going to a mountain cabin for a weekend — which is great! Get the prayer going! These three principles still apply: a biblical, historical, and cultural *perspective*; the *priority* of prayer support; and the *particulars* of formulating a prayer strategy.

Perspective

Too often, we youth workers tend to go about our planning and tack prayer on as an addendum. We make our plans and then ask God to bless them, rather than asking God to both give us the plans and bless their implementation. Most of us acknowledge how important prayer is. Then why don't we pray more? And why don't we make prayer *the* integral part of our preparations? I have found that taking the time to gain a healthy perspective is helpful here.

In the initial stages of developing a big-event prayer strategy, the biblical, historical, and cultural perspectives of the role of prayer are helpful to recount. In most cases, this is a refresher course. Biblically speaking, most of us can cite chapter and verse: "Apart from me you can do nothing" (John 15:5); "But in everything, by prayer and petition, with thanksgiving, present your requests to God" (Philippians 4:6); "If two of you on earth agree about anything you ask for, it will be done for you by my Father in heaven" (Matthew 18:19); "If you believe, you will receive whatever you ask for in prayer" (Matthew 21:22).

I find it helpful to go back over these "standard" passages on the priority of prayer and meditate on them until they seep into the inner recesses of my soul. It is also motivating and convicting to study biblical characters like Nehemiah, Jehoshaphat, or Daniel, who won battles (certainly big events!) and had an impact on nations through prayer. Such meditations and studies help narrow the gap between what we know in our heads and hearts about prayer, and what we practice on a daily basis in our own lives and ministries. These quotes explain:

> The men who have done the most for God in this world have been those who have been early on their knees.
>
> —E. M. Bounds

> The globe itself lives and is upheld as by Atlas' arms through the prayers of those whose love has not grown cold. The world lives by these uplifted hands, and by nothing else.
>
> —Helmut Thielicke

> Luther and his companions were men of such mighty pleading with God, that they broke the spell of ages, and laid nations subdued at the foot of the Cross. John Knox grasped all Scotland in his strong arms of faith and his prayers terrified tyrants. Whitefield, after much bold, faithful closet pleading, went to the devil's playground and took more than a thousand souls out of the paws of the lion in one day.
>
> —D. L. Moody

I bet you've read the biographies, too. The men and women who were used by God to shape lives and to shake the world were, almost always, men and women devoted to prayer. Often they spent *hours on their knees each morning* before the workday started. Too often we take a group of students to a big event (or hold one ourselves) that could very well change lives, with only a minimal amount of prayer support invested before or during the event. Lest we say that times were different when the biographies were written, a contemporary cultural perspective will stop that argument in its tracks.

We're told that the average Korean pastor spends from two to three hours a day in prayer. Colombian youth reportedly gather regularly by the thousands for all-night prayer vigils. Daily intercession for many, perhaps most, non-Western believers may be measured in hours rather than minutes. Those facts should motivate us to take our praying more seriously.

Priorities

Organizing a trip to a big event for your group can be a daunting task. There are students to motivate and sign up, money to raise, travel plans to make, adult sponsors to recruit, and lodging to secure. All these tasks are critical to the success of the trip. The problem comes when we allow the tasks to consume our time and energies to the detriment of mobilizing proper prayer support from church members, parents, and the students themselves.

When we find ourselves falling into this trap (and most of us do at one time or another), it is time to stop and regain perspective. We must remember what our proper priorities should be. Remember: The goal of a big-event prayer strategy is to help create an environment through prayer that will produce maximum spiritual impact in the lives of a maximum number of students in a minimum amount of time. That type of environment is created not through greater attendance, or better funding, or a classier retreat facility—but through prayer.

Particulars

It is one thing to have a healthy perspective when it comes to mobilizing prayer support for big events and to keep prayer as the top priority. It is a different matter when it comes to the practical aspects of implementing a strategy.

I have mobilized prayer support for big events when I was the guy running the event. I have also mobilized prayer for a variety of local, regional, and national big events, and served as an intercessor for many others. In each case, the strategy differed, depending on the style of the event, the creativity of the prayer mobilizers, and the pool of people from which to draw prayer support. In a local church setting (which is the most relevant to most of you), there are three strategic components of that pool to target when mobilizing prayer: parishioners, parents, and participants. Following are some practical examples of prayer mobilization within these three groups.

Parishioners

- Encourage members of your congregation to adopt a student for focused prayer before, during, and after the big event. Take digital photos of participating students and staff. Using a layout program on your computer, develop prayer cards listing relevant prayer issues at the bottom of the page. This will give intercessors a visible prayer reminder they can stick in their Bible or on the refrigerator.
- Set up a prayer clock during the event. Members of your congregation can sign up to intercede for your students and the event during set times each day. This could be twenty-four hours around the clock or whatever works best for you. For a visual reminder, make a large poster showing a clock broken down into fifteen-minute segments, with intercessors' names written in, and post it in the church fellowship hall or another visible location.
- Develop a prayer chain within your church. During the big event, you can call in current and pressing prayer concerns at regular intervals for quick prayer response.
- Utilize bulletin inserts for mobilizing prayer. List those who will be attending, relevant prayer issues, who to contact for involvement in the adoption ministry or prayer clock, and so on.
- Identify and mobilize prayer groups and individual intercessors to cover your group and the event in prayer. I have found senior citizens have a special affinity

for youth and love to pray for them. This is an excellent way to involve them in your youth ministry.

- Challenge folks in your congregation to come with you to the event with the express purpose of interceding for your group and other aspects of the event.

Parents

- Take the time to explain to parents your desires for the event and their kids. Let them know that it is not only a fun excursion, but also a potentially life-changing experience.
- Teach parents how to pray more effectively for their children—both during the event, and ongoing. (See "31 Ways to Pray for Youth" in the appendix. Moms In Touch and other groups also have excellent resources concerning this area.)
- Give them specific prayer points to guide their intercession before, during, and after the event.
- Affirm to them your commitment to pray for their children, and let them know you value their input and interaction as you partner in prayer for their children.

Participants

- Make prayer a requirement for students attending the big event as well as for their adult sponsors. Have them make a commitment to pray regularly for various aspects of the event: other students in your group, others who will be attending, speakers, musicians, and programming leaders, unsaved students, and so on.
- Divide students into prayer triplets that meet on a regular basis before, during, and after the event so that more-detailed prayer requests can be shared and time can be given to focus on those requests.

- Make united prayer a top priority in your preparatory time together.
- Train adult sponsors in prayer. Assign students to each adult for focused prayer. Teach them how to pray "on site with insight" (i.e., pray continually while allowing the unfolding dynamics of the event itself to shape prayers). Integrate united prayer into your sponsor briefings.
- Model a lifestyle of prayer. Show students, adult sponsors, and others in your congregation you are serious about making prayer foundational in this big event and in your youth ministry in general.

This is just the tip of the iceberg when it comes to creative ideas for mobilizing prayer. Let your imagination soar and allow the Holy Spirit to be your guide. Remember that the goal of your big-event prayer strategy is to help create an environment through prayer that will produce maximum spiritual impact in the lives of a maximum number of students in a minimum amount of time. With such a strategy in place, big events will reap tremendous fruit. When a prayer strategy becomes foundational in your ministry, fruitfulness will continue. The lives of many of your students will never be the same!

Postscript: On-Site Prayer Team Guidelines

Below are some guidelines I have used over the years with a variety of on-site teams. They help insure that all your team members are on the same page when you engage in your intercession. You can adjust them to fit your situation and needs. Even if you can't gather a team for your event, with a little adaptation you can mobilize your adult counselors/sponsors to serve as an ad hoc, on-site team. (Refer to the appendix for more guidelines.)

1. Preparation
   A. Check your armor (Ephesians 6:10-18).
   B. Check your character and relationships.

- Humility (2 Chronicles 7:14, 20:12)
- Compassion/empathy (Matthew 9:35-38)
- Submission (James 4:7)
- Personal sin issues (Psalm 66:18; Isaiah 59:2)
- Marriage and family life (1 Peter 3:7)
- Other relationships (John 13:34-35, 14:15-21, 17:20-23; 1 Timothy 2:8)
- Belief and faith problems

C. Check your motives. (1 Chronicles 28:9; Proverbs 16:2; 1 Corinthians 4:5; James 4:3)

2. Participation in united prayer sessions
   A. Invite His presence (Joshua 6; Chronicles 20:21-22).
   B. Request His protection (Deuteronomy 23:14; Psalms 5:11, 32:7; John 17:11,15; 2 Thessalonians 3:3).
   C. Appropriate His power.
   - Silence the enemy; subdue his influence (Matthew 10:1)
   D. Plead His promises.
   - Use the Word of God
   E. Seek His purposes.
   - Be about both seeking *and* inquiring (Joshua 9:14; Zephaniah 1:6)
   - Flow with the Spirit (Romans 8:26)
   (A key to effective intercession is allowing the Holy Spirit to conform your prayers to the will of God—discerning the mind of Christ concerning what to pray, where to pray, and when to pray. That requires much *listening* as well as speaking. Do not be afraid of silence.)

3. Positioning
   A. Each member has a function/role on the team (1 Corinthians 12).

- *Every* role is important!
- If you're a "foot" don't try to be a "hand."

B. Submission to leadership is critical to the proper functioning of the team (Hebrews 13:17).
(On-site prayer means more than gathering in a room. Include plenty of prayerwalking, praying within general sessions, praying through room accommodations. Be inclusive—don't pray through general sessions or rallies while forgetting seminars, breakout sessions, and other events.)

4. Perseverance

A. Be persistent (Luke 11:5-13; 18:1-8).

B. Pace yourself to ensure persistence.
(Intercessors can burn out from long hours and little sleep just like event leaders and sponsors/counselors.)

PART IV: THE PRAYING MOVEMENT

10. PRAYER FOR THE CAMPUS, COMMUNITY, AND CITY

There is nothing that makes us love a man so much as praying for him.

—William Law

I am 13 years old and I'm in 8th grade. Me and a friend of mine had been sharing the same feeling of wanting to encourage our classmates to be a light to our community, city, state, and nation. So this year, for the first time, our school started a program called P.U.S.H. Which most everyone knows stands for Pray Until Something Happens. We received permission from our principle, and started having a group together for prayer every Friday Morning. We only have about 10-15 minutes, but we have the time to read a [Bible] verse or short lesson, and take prayer-requests and pray. Our school is K-8 but we only allow grades 6-8 because we thought they were the only grades that could fully understand everything, with a few exceptions. But of those students, which number probably around 100, we usually have about 20. And that is pleasing for us, even though we are praying that more will eventually join us by the end of this year. We also are praying that some of our younger peers will take over this group when we go to High School. Please be in prayer for this small-town school that just wants to serve God.

—A student in North Carolina[1]

While a number of specific acts of prayer have been sprinkled through the past nine chapters, it is now (to steal a popular phrase) "Tool Time!" I don't think you need any further motivation or inspiration concerning the imperative of praying for the campus, where students spend most of their time, or the culture, where students spend *all* of their time. In today's culture, the campus is becoming less and less the epicenter of student life, but it is still our primary mission field, and we need to approach it accordingly. With that in mind, I offer a number of prayer tools that are working in a variety of venues across the country. Just remember (I know I sound like a broken record, but deal with it) to ask the Holy Spirit to help you pick out the tools that are right for you and for your ministry—don't try to use them all!

See You at the Pole

Many of us have heard of, and likely been involved with, See You at the Pole, a movement established by students who gather annually to pray at their school flagpoles at 7:00 A.M. on the third Wednesday of September. Here's how it all began:

> A small group of teenagers in Burleson, Texas, came together for a DiscipleNow weekend in early 1990. They came seeking God. Little did they know how powerfully God was about to move. On Saturday night God penetrated their hearts like never before. The students were broken before God and burdened for their friends. Compelled to pray, they drove to three different schools that night. Not knowing exactly what to do, they went to the school flagpoles and prayed for their friends, schools, and leaders. Those students had no idea how God would use their obedience.
>
> God used what He did among those teenagers and others who were holding similar prayer meetings at their schools to birth a vision in the hearts of youth leaders across Texas. The vision was that students throughout Texas would follow these examples and meet at their school flagpoles to pray simultaneously. The challenge was named See You at the Pole (SYATP)

at an early brainstorming session. The vision was shared with 20,000 students in June 1990 at Reunion Arena in Dallas, Texas.

Only God had envisioned how many students would step up to the challenge. At 7:00 A.M. on September 12, 1990, more than 45,000 teenagers met at school flagpoles in four different states to pray before the start of school.

A few months later, a group of youth ministers from all over the country gathered together for a national conference in Colorado. Many of them reported that their students had heard about the prayer movement in Texas and were equally burdened for their schools. No other events had been planned, but it was clear that students across the country would be creating their own national day of student prayer. There was no stopping them.

On September 11, 1991, at 7:00 A.M., one million students gathered at school flagpoles all over the country. From Boston, Massachusetts, to Los Angeles, California, students came together to pray. Some sang, some read Scripture, but most importantly, they prayed. Like those first students, they prayed for their schools, for their friends, for their leaders, and for their country.

As in all great movements of prayer, See You at the Pole did not begin in the hearts of people. It began in the heart of God. God used the obedience of a small group of teenagers to ignite what has become an international movement of prayer among young people.

Since 1991, See You at the Pole has grown to God-sized proportions. Within only a couple of years, students were praying in several countries around the world. Now, more than 3 million students from all 50 states participate in SYATP. Students in more than twenty countries take part. In places like Canada, Guam, Korea, Japan, Turkey, and the Ivory Coast, students are responding to God and taking seriously the challenge to pray.[2]

The See You at the Pole website, operating in conjunction with the National Network of Youth Ministries, collects testimonies from students around the world who have had profound, powerful experiences. Here are a few of their stories:

My friends and I decided to do SYATP on September 11 for obvious reasons. I arrived at the wall outside our school with a small flag about five minutes before we had planned for SYATP to start. Five minutes later we were about to start when a teacher came up and asked if anyone could join. When I said yes, she and a few other teachers and a group of students joined the circle. Then I prayed for our school year, our school, our nation and anyone who lost loved ones in the attacks on America. Then I invited anyone who wanted anything to just step forward and say whatever they wanted. One of the parents standing next to me said that she would like to take a moment to pray for all the victims' families. All this time people were joining the circle. A few teachers were standing by taking pictures. Finally after about 5 to 10 minutes we ended with the Pledge Of Allegiance that one of the gym teachers suggested we do. One of my friends told me later that lots of people were crying. The amazing part about this is that someone started to count the people there and she stopped at about 150. I wasn't expecting more than 10. Obviously God had a big part to play in this. Maybe doing SYATP on September 11 wasn't such a bad idea after all.

—A student in Rhode Island

We did SYATP a day early due to scheduling conflicts on September 18. It is not our rainy season, but it rained today. We had about 45 students and teachers who showed up. Most importantly, God showed up, and although our bodies were dampened, our spirits were not!

—A student in Nairobi, Kenya

Our school is in an area known for gangs, drugs, and violence. We all greeted each other as we gathered around our flagpole, and we began to pray. We all understood the power of prayer, as we prayed for our families, school, and fellow classmates. The 13 of us heard kids mocking us and swearing but we still kept on going. At that moment we decided to pray for those kids, knowing that one day they will have to bow down to God and give an account for their lives.

—A student in Detroit

Although most youth workers have exhorted students to view their schools as mission fields and to pray accordingly, See You at the Pole has helped to escalate school-focused prayer among students over the past decade. But it is by no means the only campus-oriented prayer strategy being utilized. Listed below are a number of additional strategies being used by students around the country and world. Most of them were first implemented in the context of a prayer group, campus Christian club, or a similar gathering of the body of Christ that meets on a regular basis on a campus. They can also be modified to work in youth groups, community or citywide gatherings, and other venues where the body of Christ is coming together in unity.

Campus Lighthouses

The Lighthouse Movement has gained significant momentum in recent years as it has been championed by the Mission America Coalition.[3] Their website explains the concept:

> The Lighthouse strategy encourages Christians everywhere to shine the Light of Jesus Christ through praying, caring and sharing . . . . A Lighthouse is a person, family, or group that commits to praying for, caring for, and then sharing Jesus Christ with their neighbors, co-workers, friends, and family members. A Lighthouse can be at home, work, school, prison . . . anywhere! As you live out the Lighthouse strategy to your neighbors, God will open doors of opportunity for you to share your faith—giving them an opportunity to know Jesus Christ.
>
> Lighthouse Christians are breaking out of the car-to-garage-to-house mold to meet and develop relationships with their neighbors. They are literally opening their doors, demonstrating Christ's love to the family next door.
>
> A Lighthouse can be a church, family, business, school group, or other gathering. Participants commit to pray regularly—by name—for their neighbors, and to develop genuine friendships that can lead to sharing the gospel.

The youth ministry version of Lighthouses, promoted by The Campus Alliance and other groups,[4] is found below, written in a manner that addresses students. You will note that this strategy contains a number of ideas that can stand alone or be utilized in different contexts.

Becoming a Campus Lighthouse

You are invited to become a Campus Lighthouse at your school! You can "let your light shine" on your campus and bring the light of Christ to your school through three powerful prayer actions:

1. First Things First

Prayer must be the first priority if you expect God to do anything significant on your campus. God promised: "Call unto me and I will answer you and show you great and mighty things which you do not know" (Jeremiah 33:3, NASB). When you call upon God, you can count on Him to do more than you ever imagined possible. You can do this when *three* friends (you and two others) meet *three* times a week to pray for *three* friends who need Christ. In every "prayer triplet," nine friends who need Christ will be prayed for! Consider starting a prayer triplet with friends from your sports team, school club, home church, or campus outreach.

2. First Light

Once a number of you are praying together in threes, make a list of each of your first-period classmates. Challenge other Christian students in your campus clubs and other groups at your school to pray in threes and *pray by name for every person* in their first-period class. Why? Because your "heart's desire and prayer to God for [them] is that they may be saved" (Romans 10:1). You and your praying friends can set the pace by praying for each person in your first-period class every week.

Think about it. Every person in your school can be prayed for by name at least once a day. First Light works best in the context of a student-led campus club of some sort, be it First Priority, Youth Alive, or a club of any other name. It will take most, if not all, of the Christian students on your campus working together on this strategy for it to work.

3. First Friday

After you begin praying in triplets and praying for everyone in your first-period class, consider fasting and praying on the first Friday of every month. The combination of prayer and fasting will help break Satan's hold on your school. When Jesus' disciples tried to help a teenager in bondage, they were powerless. Jesus told them, "This kind does not go out except by fasting and prayer" (Matthew 17:21, NASB).

While you should fast as the Lord leads, one common fast is to skip breakfast and lunch on that Friday. At some schools, students meet before school at the flagpole and pray like they do for See You at the Pole. During lunchtime, prayer triplets meet and pray.

Other Prayer Ideas

Yearbooks—Have students cut out or photocopy every picture and name from a school yearbook, paste them on cards, and distribute them throughout the community to those who would commit to praying regularly for one or more students.[5] Or, scan the photos into computers, add relevant information and ways to pray, and print out prayer cards.

Lockers—Have Christian students pray for their peers whose lockers are in close proximity to their own. For instance, pray for those five lockers to the right and five lockers to the left. Try to pray for whatever number is workable in order to cover all the lockers.

Homeroom—At some schools, each student has a "homeroom." The Christians in each homeroom can take on the rest of the students in that class as their prayer assignment. The idea is that while they are in the homeroom, they pray for the other students.

Station Theme/Banners—As a high school student in Wichita, Kansas, Brandon was ignited with a passion for prayer at a summer prayer conference his family attended. The Lord stirred him with a vision that involved prayer for his school. With little knowledge of how to go about it, Brandon gathered a few friends and started meeting weekly to pray. To guide their praying and keep them focused, they made banners that described four prayer station themes:

- *Station 1:* Pray that God will save the lost (2 Peter 3:9).
- *Station 2:* Pray that God will move in the lives of our teachers and administration (1 Timothy 2:1-2).
- *Station 3:* Pray that God will break strongholds in the school through spiritual warfare (2 Corinthians 10:4). Ask God to reveal where Satan has control. When these strongholds are identified, pray that God will break them and work freely in the school.
- *Station 4:* Pray that God will send revival (Acts 2:17).

Moving from station to station at five-minute intervals, they wrote the names of classmates and teachers on the banners, praying for them by name. God began to move powerfully at Brandon's school, and this intrepid group of "banner pray-ers" soon grew rapidly. Christian students at other schools began to adopt this or similar methods as student prayer groups multiplied throughout Wichita and other cities in Kansas.[6] A few years later, I stood next to Brandon as he cast a vision for campus prayer to more than six thousand students from around the country, and then led them in a powerful concert of prayer.

Prayerwalks—Prayerwalking (which is simply praying as you walk or, as Steve Hawthorne describes it, "praying on-site with insight") helps you stay focused while praying, and allows you to visually connect with the object of your prayer. Prayerwalks can be done alone or in groups around the perimeter of schools (also called "Jericho Walks"), through halls, or in neighborhoods. Prayerwalking can be quite creative. In a small community in my home state, a youth group met at 5 A.M. at a different school each week, driving inconspicuous stakes into the ground, with relevant Scripture written on them at each corner of the school grounds. Brandon's group would prayerwalk the school hallways and subtly anoint classroom doorposts with oil. A group of youth workers from my city was invited into the classroom of a Christian teacher while the students were at lunch. With heads up and eyes open so as to be less conspicuous, we interceded for students, teachers, and the school before prayerwalking the halls on our way out.

Prayer Clocks—Recruit students, parents, teachers, and others involved at your school or in the community to sign up to pray for your school for a ten-minute stretch each school day. If you recruit ninety-six people to pray, people will be praying for your school continuously from 6:00 A.M. until 10:00 P.M. every school day! If that seems daunting, why not get enough people to pray bell-to-bell—from the start of school to dismissal.

Thirty-Second Kneel Downs—This prayer evangelism strategy consists of students kneeling down at their schools, in front of their lockers or in another public venue, on a daily basis (the suggested time is 7:30 a.m.) for thirty seconds of focused prayer. The purpose is (1) to broaden the school prayer base, (2) to put prayer back in school, and (3) to develop students' reputation as Christians so they may freely share the gospel on campus. The time may be broken up into three segments:

- *Segment 1: God, Thanks!* "God, I bow my knee in humility to You. I know Your loving presence will be with me all day. Thank You for loving me today. I love You, too!" "Love the Lord your God with all your heart and with all your soul and with all your mind" (Matthew 22:37).
- *Segment 2: God, Touch Them!* "God, touch the teachers, administration, and students on my campus today. One touch from You, Father, can change someone's destiny. Touch them through me." "Love your neighbor as yourself" (Matthew 22:39).
- *Segment 3: God, Tell Them!* "God, the message of Jesus' love for my campus must be told. Use me as the messenger. I will tell those around me how much You love them." "Therefore go and make disciples of all nations" (Matthew 28:19).[7]

Prayer Lockers—A hallway locker can be designed as a "prayer locker" where students are invited to drop prayer requests through the slits located at the top of the locker door. Ask students who use the locker to also drop in a note when God answers their request. Then mobilize Christian students to hit their knees! When God answers these prayers, you will have not only blessed other students, but also likely increased their spiritual interest dramatically.

Prayer and Fasting—Many students are learning to fast in conjunction with prayer. A significant example is First Friday, which is a national initiative of Intercessors for America[8] and is incorporated into the Campus Lighthouse strategy mentioned earlier. The underlying purpose of combined fasting and prayer on campus is to help break Satan's hold on the school. When Jesus' disciples tried to help a young person in spiritual bondage, they were powerless. Jesus told them, "This kind does not go out except by prayer and fasting" (Matthew 17:21, NASB[9]). Students and faculty fast by skipping breakfast and lunch on the first Friday of each month, and use that time for corporate prayer for their campus.

Prayer Guides—Students are often motivated to pray, but are unsure what to pray. A succinct prayer guide that provides both the reasons behind the praying and the particulars of how to pray can be helpful. When mobilizing students to pray, don't assume anything and don't overwhelm them with too many prayer points.

Prayer Zone Partners (for Adults)—Yellow school zone signs are, by law, on the roads surrounding all public schools. Prayer Zone Partners[10] use these signs to remind folks to pray for neighboring schools every time they drive through a school zone:

> The original concept of Prayer Zone Partners came from the heart of David Mewbourne, Oklahoma district Youth Alive director. One day while David drove to work, he realized he was late and found himself stuck in a school zone. David slowed to the posted speed limit. He realized he would be delayed further because of the school zone. As he complained to himself, he experienced a "God moment"—one of those moments when God gets your attention, perhaps with information that makes you uncomfortable. God quickly reminded David of his own personal commitment to schools, students, teachers, and campus ministry. God spoke to David's heart and showed him that traveling through a school zone was an excellent time to pray for that school instead of complain about being late. From that point on in his life, David converted school zones into prayer zones.[11]

Prayer Zone Partners are best known for the yellow, diamond-shaped, static stickers that can be placed in the corner of the windshield as a reminder. The stickers can be customized to focus on an individual ministry, network, city movement, or to target a specific school. As I always say, "Change your oil, but don't change your prayer zone!"

I am going to run the risk of sounding like a broken record (a vinyl record album, that is, or perhaps a scratched CD)—and remind you again to ask the Holy Spirit to help you pick out which of these "tools" will work for your ministry. Or, even better, allow Him to help you mutilate what I have suggested above in order for it to be even *more* effective in your situation!

Notes

1. Source: http://everyschool.com
2. Source for this and the stories that follow: www.syatp.com
3. From the Mission America website, www.missionamerica.org Because these stories are continually evolving as the Spirit leads, visit the site for the latest information.
4. The Campus Alliance is a coalition of more than thirty national youth ministry denominations and organizations who have united around the mission of reaching every middle school, junior high, and high school in America. For more information go to http://everyschool.com
5. As you do this, you need to adhere to appropriate copyright laws—don't do something illegal as a prayer strategy!
6. Developed by Brandon Page and Terry Johnson of Wichita, Kansas, and cited by Cheri Fuller in *When Teens Pray* (Sisters, Ore.: Multnomah, 2002), p. 17. Other details through personal correspondence.
7. Source: www.30kd.org
8. For more information about First Fridays, go to the website for Intercessors for America: www.ifapray.org
9. See www.youthalive.ag.org/ya_pz_whatis.cfm for more information.
10. Source: www.prayerzonepartners.com
11. Source: www.youthalive.ag.org/ya_pz_history.cfm

11. PRAYER FOR THE NATION(S)

You can have a thrilling role in reaping God's harvest. Only a small percentage of God's people are actually involved in seed sowing, watering, cultivating, and preparing more harvesters, yet all of us could participate on a deeper level than we have ever dreamed. If you are willing, prayer offers you a way to be significantly involved in world harvest.

—Wesley Duewel

A few decades ago, only the occasional student would venture out on a "short-term missions trip" during the summer. These days, missions trips are pretty standard youth ministry fare, as is a wider focus on missions in general. Most of us in youth work recognize the value of giving kids cross-cultural missions experiences, be it across town, across the continent, or across the ocean. The benefits of such trips are innumerable. Such experiences can be, and often are, life transforming. Stories like Linsey's below are the norm rather than the exception!

A few years ago we took a team to Macedonia on a summer missions trip. The first day we arrived in Skopje, the group entered into a time of intercession. As we were asking God for souls, for divine appointments, and for His blessing on the day's outreach, a teen leader named Linsey was led to read Acts 16. It spoke of a woman named Lydia who responded to Paul's message and became the first convert in Asia. Linsey, who had never led anyone to Christ, prayed, "God, give me my Lydia! Give me a person today whom I can lead into the kingdom of God."

Hours later the team was ministering in a park downtown. As Linsey looked throughout the crowd, her heart was drawn to a woman who seemed very interested in the dramas and testimonies that were being given. Sitting down by the woman, she began to share her faith. After some minutes, the woman responded to Linsey's appeal and dedicated her life to Jesus. As the two were parting some time later, Linsey asked for the woman's name and address. She replied, "My name is Lydia." Linsey almost fainted with joy as she thought about God's answer to prayer. Just as in Paul's day, this Macedonian Lydia was Linsey's and the YWAM team's first convert in the nation of Macedonia. Many others followed.[1]

Just as going on missions trips helps us get a more holistic view of "for God so loved the world" (John 3:16) missions praying (praying for the nations) serves a similar function. Following are a few ways to help your ministry and your students engage in such praying. Included is information from several websites. Remember that web-based prayer material is changing so rapidly that anything I list could be dated or enhanced significantly by the time you read this. But I'll take a shot at it anyway:

The World Prayer Team — This web prayer strategy is based at The World Prayer Center in Colorado Springs, Colorado.

The Apostle Paul's epistles truly were delivered by snail mail — by the time recipients in the Christian communities were greeted by his letter carriers, Paul's prayer requests may have been a bit dated. Today technology provides for prayer requests at the speed of Internet transmission. And the World Prayer Center is this era's global clearinghouse for prayer requests, linking the World Prayer Team comprised of Christians around the globe.

"Hundreds of thousands of praying people at home and in church-based prayer centers will take up the burdens of those who send in their requests, as well as focus prayer on targeted areas," testifies their website. "Real-time posting" means prayers are offered as needs are entered on the website. Confidentiality is provided as needed for those who require anonymity and protection from religious or family persecution.

The World Prayer Center and its World Prayer Team also provide "prayer journeys to key world locations; enable churches to share needs with their own congregations and the world" through "prayer kiosks and customized prayer portals"; and promotes the center to nonChristians, encouraging them to come to the site for prayer. "The goal of the World Prayer Team is to enlist millions of people around the world, to pray for the requests posted on the website."[2]

Intercessors for America (IFA) — For more than thirty years this ministry has been helping folks pray with insight and accuracy for our nation.[3] A few years ago they launched a Young Intercessors for America (YIFA) branch. Their website is jammed with wonderful resources to help praying people of all ages intercede for our country.[4] IFA also has a special emphasis on prayer for those in authority (1 Timothy 2:1-2).[5]

The Call and Elijah Revolution — You may be familiar with The Call, which held daylong prayer and fasting gatherings at various sites over the first several years of the new millennium. These events brought groups ranging in size from tens to hundreds of thousands in Washington, D.C., Boston, Kansas City, and a number of other cities. The Call model, championed by prophetic youth leader Lou Engle, is also being used overseas to call emerging generations together for seasons of prayer and fasting. The Call website (www.thecall-revolution.com) as well as Lou Engle's sister site (www.elijahrevolution.com) offer a variety of radical prayer and fasting resources, ideas, and ministry opportunities.

Adopting Unreached People Groups—A number of missions organizations, such as the U.S. Center for World Missions,[6] offer opportunities to adopt peoples that have not yet had a chance to hear and respond to the gospel message—a wonderful project for a youth group. USCWM's "Adopt-A-People Campaign" strategy involves the following:

> A church congregation or fellowship group makes a serious commitment to do all they can to reach their adopted people group by working in partnership with the mission agency of their choice. All adopting churches agree to provide informed, concerted prayer for their people. Depending on the mission agency chosen, a church may also be asked to help fund the effort to reach their people or supply personnel to help reach them.[7]

Praying Through the Window—This has been rightly described as the largest focused, sustained prayer initiative in history. Missiologists have long known that the majority of unreached people groups are located in a rectangular-shaped "window" that extends from 10 degrees north to 40 degrees south of the equator, stretching across North Africa, the Middle East, India, and Asia and encompassing the majority of the world's Muslims, Hindus, and Buddhists. Ted Haggard writes:

> Research shows that while 97 percent of the people who live in the least-evangelized countries are located in the 10/40 Window, about one percent of missions funding is spent there. Why is this so? Churches and mission agencies answer, "We can't effectively work there." The spiritual, political, and economic realities of the 10/40 Window seem overwhelming. We need a spiritual breakthrough.[8]

In the early 1990s, a number of missions groups and prayer mobilizers collaborated to raise up unprecedented prayer for this part of the world. Prayer maps, prayer guides, and a host of other resources were made available to the church. Hundreds of thousands of churches and youth ministries participated in this prayer initiative; organizers make a conservative estimate that tens of millions of believers united in prayer for this initiative. C. Peter Wagner describes the result:

> For ten years we who have joined hands in the worldwide prayer movement and in the International Spiritual Warfare Network have fervently been praying for the unreached peoples of the 10/40 Window. . . . As a result of focused prayer, the evangelistic momentum in the 10/40 Window is at an all-time high. True, there are more unreached people groups to reach and many more churches to be planted, but God has raised up an incredible body of workers to move in, and certainly the prayer momentum in the 10/40 Window will continue escalating. Latin America has revival fires burning brightly. Asia is experiencing the greatest evangelistic harvest in the world. Africa south of the Sahara is now majority Christian. Revival reports are coming from virtually every part of the world.[9]

In the last few years, a new prayer target, the 40/70 Window, has been identified and a similar prayer mobilization effort is under way. Wagner says Global Harvest is responding to God's call for a worldwide prayer and spiritual warfare initiative focusing on the 40/70 Window during a five-year period ending in 2005. He states:

> Given the maturity of the global prayer movement, I believe we will see as much change in the spiritual atmosphere of the 40/70 Window in five years as we saw in the 10/40 Window in ten years. If we can see spiritual breakthroughs in Latin America, I have faith to believe that we will also see breakthrough in Spain and Poland and Russia and Uzbekistan and Yugoslavia and Switzerland and Italy and in many others nations of the 40/70 Window.[10]

24-7 — This U.K.-based prayer ministry has exploded worldwide over the past few years.

A report on the movement in *Religion Today* summarized the 24-7 program. This movement has gained much "spiritual traction." Recently 24-7 pray-ers engage in round-the-clock, nonstop prayer, using the 1700s Moravian Revival in Germany as their basis. Young people congregate in "Boiler Rooms," praying in shifts, around the clock, often up to a month at a time. Youth worldwide, especially in Europe (Germany, Sweden, France, Switzerland, Spain, Scotland, Ireland, England, and Wales) and also in Ecuador, Australia, and the United States are involved in this movement. Coordinator Pete Grieg describes the atmosphere in the prayer rooms as "heavenly":

> People experience God in a new way and learn to relate to Him personally, as a Father. An hour feels like 10 minutes in God's presence, and prayers often are answered swiftly. Participants sometimes paste written prayers, poems, artwork, and spiritual graffiti on the walls.
>
> "The prayer room in Northampton [England] is mad, crazy, outrageous, contagious, deep, real—we can hardly describe it," one participant wrote. "God is really here. We walked into the room and could 'feel' God's presence, almost as if something was brushing against your skin."
>
> Twenty-four/seven prayer rooms aren't just in churches. They are in skate parks, deserted buildings, farmhouses, even nightclubs. For this generation, the mission field is the clubs and the skate parks. Holiness that is divorced from the world is not Jesus' model of holiness, which is to go to parties, make children laugh, and confuse the religious culture. The goal is to turn the tide in youth culture. . . .
>
> "There is a sense that God is doing this and we are running to catch up."[11]

Partly because this movement is so new, and partly because it is primarily driven by emerging generations, 24-7 is somewhat unstructured and free-flowing, and at times radical. Yet behind it is a biblical and mature vision: "24-7 exists to transform the world through a movement of Christ-centered and missions-minded prayer."[12] See the appendix for the values of the 24-7 movement; they reflect spiritual maturity and should be considered by emerging prayer movements of any size and scope. Also visit their website. It's loaded with resources, stories, and more: www.24-7prayer.com

The concept of 24-7 can be easily adapted to most church or ministry situations. Not long after I read *Red Moon Rising*, the account of the beginnings of the 24-7 movement, I told my pastor about this unique initiative. He immediately procured a copy of the book for himself and read it cover-to-cover in the space of a few days. Soon, our church was setting up a prayer room and mobilizing twenty-four hours of prayer during Easter weekend. The trouble was, too many people wanted to join in! We eventually ended up with ninety-six hours of prayer that weekend, and a room with Scripture, poetry, and art covering the walls. Tim soon shared our experience at our city's monthly clergy gathering. A number of other churches have now caught the vision, and 24-7 prayer is now happening in our community of twelve thousand for an entire week each month!

A Few Other Hot Sites
As of the time of this writing, these sites have some pretty insightful information and are worth checking out:
- *Youth Arise.* www.youtharise.com, an Australian-based youth prayer movement
- *Youth Prayer Week.* www.youthprayerweek.com, an initiative of the Youth Commission of the World Evangelical Alliance
- *Connect Europe.* www.connecteurope.org, a network of emerging young European prayer leaders
- *The Coaching Center Prayer Ideas.* www.gocampus.org/ contains various campus-oriented prayer helps and resources for students.

Choose Your Own

I could continue with more examples of great strategies, ideas, and the like to help young people pray for their nation and the nations of the world. But the Internet is exploding with creative ideas; just use a good search engine to find the most current resources. Go for it! For example, www.thecry.ca/cry.swf details the emergence of the CRY (Canadian Revived Youth) movement in Ottawa, Canada, which began in August 2002. This letter shares the enthusiasm of a Canadian high school student who attended:

> Wow! I'm more than encouraged to read what God is doing in schools across the globe! I've home schooled all my life, and just this year (my grade eleven year) God told me to go to school. He laid a particular high school on my heart, and told me to go to that school. This school has the worst ratings in Ottawa for drugs, suicides, and all of Satan's other tools. I had never, not once heard anything good about this school until God opened the doors for me to go and placed me in that school! Well . . . I'm in the school now, and God put me there for a purpose. Just this past weekend, we had a drama presentation called *Heaven's Gates and Hell's Flames* at our church, and I invited like two hundred people from my school. To my surprise, like thirty of them (or so) showed up, and I know for a fact that one and possibly two of them committed their lives to the Lord, and I know without a doubt in my heart that the others that didn't make a commitment there will before the end of the year!
>
> God has revealed to me two visions about Canada. . . . We had a nation wide prayer meeting on Aug. 24th on Parliament Hill here in Ottawa. It was called THE CRY. . . . When I was praying on the hill, I looked toward the peace tower, and saw it differently than I ever had in my life! There were sets of scaffold about a quarter to a third of the way up the center of the tower. God revealed to me that the peace tower represents our nation and that the scaffold represented the *reconstruction* that God is doing in our nation. But there was one problem, and that was that there were no workers on the scaffold, and what God was saying is that the

harvest is ready (God is ready to do the construction), but the labourers are few (God wants us to reach our schools/friends). . . . I really believe that God is starting something here in Ottawa, the nation's capital, which is going to echo right across Canada! And let's not limit ourselves . . . this is going to echo right across the globe! I'm so pumped about what God's got in store! Students/brothers and sisters in Christ/friend/and whoever else, remember this, Jesus loves you, and died for you, the least you could do is stand up for Him at your schools and make a difference! If every Christian young person that goes to school stood up for what they believed in and went all out for Christ, just think of what God would do! The labourers would be so many that the construction would be done within a matter of no time at all! Just remember one other thing though, and that is that nothing is going to happen unless we commit everything to God and pray! Prayer is Power! Prayer works! Prayer makes all the difference in the world! Pray! If you're going to school on the bus, pray! If you're in gym class playing sports, pray! If you're talking to a teacher, pray! Whatever you are doing, pray! If we commit our schools to prayer, then God will move in our schools!

—A student in Ottawa, Ontario, Canada[13]

Notes

1. Personal email correspondence from Ron Boehme of Youth With A Mission, July 2003.
2. From the World Prayer Team website, www.worldprayerteam.org
3. www.ifapray.org
4. www.yifa.org/
5. See the appendix at the end of the book for "30 Ways to Pray for People in Authority."
6. www.uscwm.org
7. Source: www.adopt-a-people.org
8. Source: www.calebproject.org

9. Source: www.globalharvest.org/index.asp?action=target4070
10. www.globalharvest.org
11. *Religion Today*, June 16, 2000.
12. Peter Greig and Dave Roberts, *Red Moon Rising* (Lake Mary, Fla.: Relevant Books, 2003), p. 254.
13. Source http://everyschool.com/story_archive.cfm?StartRow=17&PageNum=5

12. THE BIG PICTURE

The great people of the earth today are the people who pray—not those who talk about prayer; nor those who say they believe in prayer; nor those who can explain about prayer; but those who take time to pray.

—S. D. Gordon

A couple of years ago my wife convinced me to allow a doctor to turn a slicing machine loose on my eyeballs. Some call it LASIK laser eye surgery, but as far as I'm concerned, my former description is quite apt. I've even got a video of the procedure. They sliced the top off my eyeballs, shot a laser at my corneas, and flipped the top back on. It was relatively painless to experience, but watching the video afterward made me wonder what in the world I had done.

What I had done was correct my myopia. *The American Heritage Dictionary* defines myopia as: "(1) A visual defect in which distant objects appear blurred because their images are focused in front of the retina rather than on it; nearsightedness. Also called short sight. (2) Lack of discernment or long-range perspective in thinking or planning."[1]

Myopia had been my lot in life since sixth grade, when rather suddenly I realized I couldn't see where the golf ball was landing. My optometrist stuck me with the style of glasses that are sold today with a mustache attached underneath. After peer ridicule destroyed my fragile pre-adolescent psyche, I begged my parents for contact lenses, and wore them pretty much nonstop until the laser surgery. Since then, I haven't had to worry about packing contact lenses, cases, and solutions or dry, itching eyes on long flights, or glasses that sit crooked on my face because I sat on them. Very, very cool!

I've been doing youth ministry for most of my (so-called) adult life because I remain rather passionate about it. Just because I am plucking an increasing number of silver hairs out of my mustache doesn't mean that I'm ready to take a demotion to a non-youth ministry position. I love youth, I love youth workers, and I love hanging out with both groups. However, when one spends that many years with one ministry focus, one runs the risk of becoming a bit myopic about it all. To be honest, that has been the case with me at times. I think youth ministry in general has got a touch of myopia as well.

Myopia: An Occupational Hazard

Let me give you a few examples. A statistic that is frequently used by youth ministry proponents is *90 percent of those who do not become Christians by the age of twenty never do.* Here is another spin on the same theme: *90 percent of those who become Christians do so by the age of twenty.* Although I did not do all that well in college statistics, I know these two statements are not saying the same thing; however, they are in the same ballpark. They convey urgency to ministry with youth.

But statisticians also tell us that most people make their decision between ages four and fourteen. That means more folks make decisions for Christ *before* their teen years than *during* junior high and high school.

And here's a quote we often use when advocating the strategic nature of youth ministry: "Historically, revivals have almost always begun among youth." True? Yes. But it can also be misleading. Revivals have, indeed, almost always begun among youth, but "youth" in this case refers to those in their teens *and* early twenties. Teenagers who fit into today's "youth ministry" category—junior high and high school students—certainly have been part of the picture, but collegians have likely had, as a whole, a *more* influential role.

My point in saying this is not to disparage youth ministry. Statistics still point to the strategic nature of youth work. One could likely make an excellent case that the *discipling* of youth, to solidify decisions made in preadolescence, should be an urgent priority. Adolescence statistically is still the last, best chance to see folks come to Christ. Many prophetic individuals and intercessors (not just youth workers) sense that secondary school campuses will be the seedbed for the next major spiritual awaking in America. I agree. These statistics have caused me to view what I do a little less myopically and a little more holistically. Just as ministry myopia is an occupational hazard in youth work, intercessory myopia is also a danger to those of us in the youth prayer movement.

Panoramic Snapshots
Steve Hawthorne accurately called See You at the Pole the largest united prayer gathering (albeit in widespread venues) in history. And the spiritual reverberations emanating from the five- to six-figure attendances at The Call events held in the United States and around the world will be felt for a very long time. But these prayer movements, and others like them within our range of vision, are just the tip of the iceberg when it comes to how God is stirring His people to pray.

But it may not even be very accurate to call them the tip of the iceberg. They may seem so to you and me, but I think it's safe to say that the majority of the world has not even heard of See You at the Pole or The Call. For believers in Colombia, the "tip of the iceberg" is likely the tens of thousands who gather for all-night united prayer *every month*. In Nigeria, the "tip" may be the millions who have gathered *at one venue* for united prayer. Who knows what "tips" may emerge in the future around the world.

I have even hesitated to include the above examples here, because by the time this book makes it to print, they could well be rendered obsolete by other amazing works of God. See You at the Pole may be eclipsed by See You Somewhere Else. Praying through the 10/40 Window may be overshadowed by Praying through the 40/70 Window or some other global prayer initiative. For all we know, the most strategic prayer movement in the history of the world may well be taking place in the countless underground home churches that are spreading throughout China, or among the pastors' prayer groups that are multiplying throughout India.[2] And we must also be reminded that size does not necessarily equate to spiritual significance. The research of George Otis Jr. shows that transformational movements often start with a literal handful of praying people.[3]

A Full Bowl

There are a few fascinating passages in the book of Revelation that give us a correct perspective:

> And when he had taken it, the four living creatures and the twenty-four elders fell down before the Lamb. Each one had a harp and they were holding golden bowls full of incense, which are the prayers of the saints.
>
> —5:8

> Another angel, who had a golden censer, came and stood at the altar. He was given much incense to offer, with the prayers of all the saints, on the golden altar before the throne. The smoke of the incense, together with the prayers of the saints, went up before God from the angel's hand.
>
> —8:3-4

These passages, in context, have much to offer. But the biblical imagery I see is that our prayers—large and small, lengthy and short, articulate and unspoken, passionate and perfunctory—are coming together in some profoundly spiritual way that is beyond our understanding. They please God as a fragrant offering, and they release His purposes on the earth. Heavenly bowls are filled with the prayers of intercessors both great and small.

I have a feeling that the bowl-filling capacity of a prayer, or prayers, is not measured by human criteria. We *all* contribute to the fullness of the bowls, as have the believers who have offered up their prayers throughout history, and as will future believers. Our prayers—and the prayers of our students—are in these bowls of heaven. They are making history as they hasten the coming of the kingdom—and the King.

Note as well that in Revelation 5:8, the twenty-four elders are holding not just bowls full of incense; they are also holding harps. Dick Eastman comments,

> Interestingly, the worshipers coming before the Lamb with harps in one hand (symbols of worship) and bowls in the other (symbols of prayer and intercession) seem to combine these two symbols in the release of a song never sung before. It is a song of global harvest.[4]

Imagine the impact if the young people in our ministries today, youth who seem to have a relatively newfound love of worship, might be the first generation to fully engage in this "harp and bowl" intercessory worship. Eastman continues:

> Later, in Revelation 8:1-6, we see "the prayers of all the saints" (a picture of intercession) being released with "much incense" (a picture of worship) at the throne. This release results in the final unfolding of God's plan through the sounding of seven trumpets, the last of which sounds a blast that releases a shout in heaven, declaring, "The kingdom of the world has become the kingdom of our Lord and of his Christ, and he will reign for ever and ever" (Revelation 11:15).

However we might interpret all this, we can be certain that worship-saturated intercession will be a key to the last great harvest on earth.[5]

At the time of this writing, the Downtown House of Prayer, a nondescript building in the heart of Portland, is home to exciting prayer and worship sessions for more than fifty hours a week. A map showing the location of every school in the city hangs on the wall and gives the DHOP-ers targets for their praying. Although involvement in DHOP is multigenerational, the more intense sessions involve young people. Similar models are emerging in cities worldwide. Perhaps some of the kids in your youth group are powerful intercessory worshipers and pray-ers. Almighty God is setting the stage before His throne. He is calling forth this generation, our generation, to be circumcised in our hearts and to cut away our carnal nature. He is calling us to be holy as He is holy, and to mentor youth to be the same.

A Call to Pray and Obey

I was cruising down the road toward another ministry assignment, listening to a taped message by Larry Lea from a recent National Symposium on the Post-denominational Church. His message was titled "Releasing the Prayer Anointing." The highlight was when he described a meeting with Paul Yonggi Cho, who pastors the largest church in the world—a "little" cell-based congregation of around eight hundred thousand in South Korea. Larry had the chance to meet this Pastor Cho, and was told in advance that he would have a grand total of twenty seconds to ask him any question. When the time finally arrived, Larry blurted out something profound like, "What did you do to build such a large church?" To which Pastor Cho replied, "Pray and obey. Ha Ha Ha Ha Ha!" And then he walked away. Classic. After feeling rather slighted, Lea realized the simple yet profound nature of Cho's comment. As I listened to the tape, I realized it as well.

Pray and Obey

Pastoring youth, serving with a youth organization, volunteering at your local church, or working at any job—it all boils down to the praying and obeying, doesn't it? Yes, I know that the multi-faceted Christian experience can't be reduced to that—Bible study, memorization and meditation, fellowship, fasting, corporate worship, and sharing one's faith are integral and essential components. But doesn't living the Christian life depend to a large extent on hearing from God and living in obedience to what you hear?

Life can get out of control for most of us. My ministry is essentially a one-man operation. I find that keeping up with everything is quite a challenge—at times nearly more than I can manage. Newsletters from a variety of ministries, most of which I am quite interested in reading, sit in a sizeable stack that only grows taller. My "to be filed" drawer in my desk overflowed, so I bought a wire basket, overflowed that, overflowed a second one, and I'm now on my third basket. Phone calls and emails don't get returned quite as quickly as I would like; important notes for messages get lost in the multiple piles that have taken over my work space. I've got places to go, people to meet, ministry to do! In the midst of all this, I have come to the realization that my own gifting—I like to do multiple tasks and keep lots of balls up in the air—is not always an asset. One can only juggle so many balls before a few start hitting the ground.

Your life agenda is likely fleshed out far differently than mine. But I sense we all, at times, share in this frustration. So what's a person to do? Buy yet another wire basket? I don't think so. I know that the answer is more complex than what I am going to write next, but . . ."pray and obey." Get marching orders daily from the Father, and obey them. That is quite simple to write or say and very difficult to carry out. I don't know about Pastor Cho, but I hear that Korean pastors spend an average of two hours a day in prayer. I would imagine that Cho logs more than the average time on his knees. That's rather convicting to me. The Koreans may have overflowing "to-be-filed" baskets as well, but when one logs that much time with the Father, passions, priorities, and personal schedules become much clearer.

I want to be about the Father's business. I do not want to be about Mike's business. Sometimes the two are the same, sometimes not. Regardless, *unless* I get my marching orders directly from the Source, I can only *hope* the former is the case. And at this point in our hectic lives, at this point in history, at this point in our toils to reach emerging generations of youth for Christ, we do not have the luxury of hoping for a match. None of us do. As someone once said, "There is always enough time to do God's will."

"Pray and obey" also applies in significant ways to what I do on assignment, be it speaking to youth workers or students, facilitating a prayer summit, consulting with an organization, or coordinating our local youth movement. I want to help youth workers and young people become men and women who know their Bibles, teach and practice biblical truth, share their faith, and live as light and salt in a dark, tasteless world. But if there is one persistent passion in what I do, if there is one persistent passion in what any of us who work with youth do, it should be to pray and obey.

And one more thing: "Ha Ha Ha Ha Ha!" A few laughs is very good therapy.

Notes

1. The American Heritage Dictionary, version 3.0.1 for Macintosh.
2. This one should catch the attention of us youth worker types, because the population of this country will soon top one billion, the majority of whom are age sixteen or younger!
3. George Otis, *Informed Intercession* (Ventura, Calif.: Renew Books, 1999). See chapter 2 for more on this.
4. Dick Eastman, *Heights of Delight* (Ventura, Calif.: Regal Books, 2002), p. 28.
5. Eastman, pp. 28-29.

APPENDIX:
MORE TOOLS FOR YOUR MINISTRY

I recently had a colonoscopy, which gave me an insider's view (literally) of my own appendix. Doctors say this tiny "attachment" has little if any purpose. Well, this appendix may be an "attachment," but it does serve a purpose. I am including in this section some stuff that doesn't seem to fit into the flow of the rest of the book. But I think it will be helpful for you and your students. So check it out.

Model Prayers

There have been more than a few times during bedtime prayers when my children, exhausted from a full day of roaming the neighborhood and evangelizing most of their friends, have begun: "Dear Jesus, thank You for this food . . . oops, I mean, thank You for this day!" No, I don't feed my kids food at bedtime. They are tired, so they revert to the prayer that is most familiar to them. I'm sure many of us have done the same thing. Now I don't want my kids to grow up praying mindless prayers, but there is a lesson to be learned in this: We tend to repeat or imitate what is familiar to us. As I have prayed with my children over the years, I have noticed that they tend to use the same phrases that Mom and Dad use. I don't think they are consciously aware of it, but they are imitating our praying.

Listed below is a variety of what I call "model prayers." They are topical, they are focused, and they are probably a little wordier than what you are used to praying. But if you read them, study them, and maybe even memorize them, you will find that your own prayers begin to take on their character and content. Feel free to adapt them for youth or for yourself.

A Morning Prayer

Father, as I begin another day I honor You as my Lord and give You praise as a God who is all-powerful and all-knowing, yet is also loving, compassionate, and merciful. Thank You that You chose me, that I am united with Christ and the recipient of every spiritual blessing in Him. Thank You for the assurance of both eternal life and abundant life. This morning I choose to follow Christ and to put to death the sinful desires of the flesh. Please fill me and empower me with Your Holy Spirit, giving me the power to resist sin and live an obedient and victorious life today. In the name of Jesus I reject the lies, deceit, and deception of Satan and his demons, and by faith put on the full armor of God that I might stand firm against him. I ask You, God, to direct my steps today so that I might live in a way that is pleasing to You. Make me sensitive to the promptings of Your Spirit, give me the courage and faith to respond to His leading, and use me as You desire to advance Your kingdom among my family and friends, on my campus, and in my world. In the mighty name of Jesus, amen.

An Evening Prayer

Thank You, Father, for Your faithfulness to me this day. Thank You for the precious gift of life in Christ, and for the indwelling power of the Holy Spirit that makes joyful, victorious living possible. As my day ends, I ask Your Holy Spirit to bring to my mind those ways in which I have grieved and quenched the Spirit by my thoughts and actions. (*Pause and listen.*) I confess these to You now. (*Confession—be brutally specific!*)

Thank You for Your promise of forgiveness and cleansing. I receive it now in Jesus' name and commit myself to seeking victory over these areas in the power of the Holy

Spirit. As I sleep, I ask You to guard and protect my body, mind, dreams, and thoughts from the schemes of the enemy. Lord, let me reside this night in Your stronghold. Keep me in the shelter of Your care. Give rest to both my body and my mind, that I may awaken refreshed and ready to love You unreservedly and serve You obediently and faithfully. In the name of Jesus I pray, amen.

A Prayer of Resistance against Spiritual Attack

Heavenly Father, You are my Refuge and my Rock. You are in control of everything that happens in my life. I am Your servant, called by Your name. Thank You for giving me the helmet of salvation—my identity in Your Son is secure. Nothing can separate me from Your love. Thank You for forgiving and cleansing my guilt. (*Proceed with any needed confession.*) I put on Your breastplate of righteousness. Holy Spirit, search out and bring into the light any schemes of darkness directed at me. I take up the shield of faith to stand against the works of the evil one. In Jesus' name, I stand on the truth of the Word of God: "The reason the Son of God appeared was to destroy the devil's work" (1 John 3:8).

Satan, I resist you in the authority of Jesus Christ. In His name I declare your works in my life destroyed. Jesus triumphed over you in the wilderness, on the cross, and in the grave. His resurrection has sealed your fate. I triumph over you now in the strength of His name. I resist and rebuke your efforts to oppress, afflict, or deceive me. I remove from you, in the name of Jesus, the right to rob me of the joy and fruit of my salvation. Through the power of the blood of Calvary, I command all powers of darkness assigned to me, sent to me, or surrounding me now to leave and go where Jesus Christ orders you to go.

Almighty God, please extend Your shield of protection over me. May Your glory follow after me as a rear guard. Send Your angels to protect me. Thank You, in Jesus' name, amen.

A Prayer for Overcoming Habitual Sin

Father, I come to You in the name of the Lord Jesus. You are the Master of my life. I am devoted to You, in love with You, abandoned to You, and committed to worshiping You, adoring You, living in obedience to You, and serving You from now throughout all eternity. You alone are the source of my joy, my contentment, my fulfillment, my peace, and the power to live my life in a manner pleasing to You. You alone possess the power and authority that I can appropriate to continually put to death my fleshly nature and live victoriously. I acknowledge that apart from You I can do nothing.

I am so aware that I am the recipient of a great measure of Your mercy, for You have chosen to bless me despite my persistent, consistent struggles with *(name habitual sin here)*. My struggle is so much a part of the fabric of my life, and has been for so many years, that it is hard to imagine gaining complete victory over it. It has infiltrated not only what I do for You, but my very being. It is most always in my thoughts, bullying its way into my devotions, my prayer life, my thoughts at night and during the day.

For many years and in many ways I have tried to justify, rationalize, or otherwise trivialize my sin. Today I must draw the line and call sin what it is—sin. I know my behavior greatly saddens You; it quenches the Spirit; it thwarts Your purposes for me; it opens me up for demonic bondage. I confess this sin to You. As I do so, I renounce all counterfeit control exercised over me in this area by my own flesh and by the adversary, who has sought to keep me in bondage. I acknowledge the self-deception that has been my consistent companion. There is no way to justify or rationalize my bondage as anything other than plain sin. As I confess this sin, I proclaim my desire to submit to Your authority in this area, as well as in every other area of my life. I take full responsibility for my sin. I confess any lying, deceit, and deception that I have employed in order to cover it up from others. I further disown, in the name of Jesus, any emotional and/or psychological influences in this bondage, as I have great fear concerning my ability to gain victory over it and live without it. I disown any genetic influence that may come through my parents. And I break and tear down, in the name of Jesus, the demonic strongholds that have been erected in my life and my ministry because of my habitual sin.

Lord, forgive me of compromise. I ask You for the courage to approach the pulling down of strongholds without reluctance or willful deception in my heart. By the power of the Holy Spirit and in the name of Jesus, I bind the satanic influences that have reinforced compromise and sin with me. I submit myself to the light of the Spirit of Truth to expose the stronghold of sin within me. By the mighty weapons of the Spirit and the Word, I proclaim that this stronghold in my life is coming down! I purpose, by the grace of God, to have only one stronghold within me: the stronghold of the presence of Christ!

I thank You, Lord, for forgiving and cleansing me from all my sins. And by the grace of God, I commit myself to follow through in this area until even the ruins of this stronghold are removed from my mind! Thank You, Father. In Jesus' name, amen.

A Prayer of Victory

Heavenly Father, I praise You that Satan is a defeated foe. I rejoice that his defeat was accomplished by the Lord Jesus Christ in His sinless life, His death, burial, resurrection, and ascension into glory. I look forward to that day when the Lord Jesus Christ rules, while Satan is bound in the bottomless pit. I rejoice that You have given to me, in my union with Christ, complete victory over Satan today.

I enter into my victory aggressively and claim my place as more than a conqueror through Him that loved me. I refuse to admit continuing defeat by Satan in any area of my life. He cannot and will not rule over me. I am dead with Christ to his rule. I affirm that the grace and mercy of God rule in all areas of my life through my union with Christ. Grant to me the grace to affirm Your victory even when experiences of life seem to say otherwise.

I thank You for these battles and all that You are seeking to accomplish in Your wisdom and design for my life. I accept the battle and rejoice in Your purpose. I willingly accept and desire to profit from all Your purposes in letting Satan's kingdom reach me. I reject all of Satan's purpose. Through the victory of my Lord and Savior I stand resolute and strong upon the certainty of my victory. In confidence I look to You, Lord Jesus. When Your purpose for this trial is fulfilled, I know that it shall fade into the dimness of forgotten battles and a defeated enemy. Through the precious name of the Lord Jesus Christ, it shall be so. Amen.

A Prayer for the Campus

Heavenly Father, I thank You for the privilege of serving as Your ambassador on my campus. You have called me to be a missionary among my friends and peers, to live as light and salt among them and share the good news of the gospel when the opportunity arises. Holy Spirit, empower and enable me and others at my school who are called by Your name to live our lives in a way worthy of our calling as children of God so that others may see Christ in us.

Lord of the harvest, I ask You to raise up workers for the harvest on our campus. Give us love and unity among ourselves, and a vision for how You want to use us to reach our campus for Christ. Help us to see others on our campus who do not know Christ through Your eyes. Protect us from the schemes of the enemy who seeks to divide us and render us ineffective.

I acknowledge that my mission field is also a battlefield, and I enter into the battle with the full armor of God, armed with the weapons of the Word of God and prayer. In the name and authority of the Lord Jesus Christ, I stand against the ploys of the enemy to keep my friends and peers blinded to the gospel. I ask you, Lord, to break Satan's power on my campus. I bind the schemes of the enemy in the name of Jesus, and I invite You, Holy

Spirit, to work in power to remove all obstacles preventing the gospel from being spread through my campus. God, open the eyes of my classmates to the light of the gospel! Bring a conviction of sin among the unconverted! May the plentiful harvest, which Your Word says exists on my campus, become a reality as You rescue many from the kingdom of darkness and bring them into the kingdom of the Son, in whose name I pray. Amen.

31 Biblical Prayers for Youth[1]

By Dick Eastman, International President of Every Home for Christ, www.ehc.org

1. **Pray for a spirit of Humility.** "The willingness to submit" (James 4:10).
2. **Pray for a spirit of Reverence.** "The fear of the Lord" (Proverbs 9:10).
3. **Pray for a spirit of Purity.** "A desire to be clean" (Matthew 5:8).
4. **Pray for a spirit of Purpose.** "A wisdom to set goals" (Proverbs 4:25).
5. **Pray for a spirit of Simplicity.** "A lifestyle uncluttered" (Romans 12:8).
6. **Pray for a spirit of Commitment.** "A dedication to the 'cause'" (Joshua 24:15).
7. **Pray for a spirit of Diligence.** "A willingness to work hard" (2 Peter 1:5).
8. **Pray for a spirit of Servanthood.** "The ministry of helps" (Galatians 6:9-10).
9. **Pray for a spirit of Consistency.** "The quality of faithfulness" (James 1:8).
10. **Pray for a spirit of Assurance.** "A depth of faith" (Hebrews 10:22).
11. **Pray for a spirit of Availability.** "A willingness to go" (Isaiah 6:8).
12. **Pray for a spirit of Loyalty.** "A zeal for fidelity" (Ruth 1:16).
13. **Pray for a spirit of Sensitivity.** "Openness of heart" (Luke 10:30-37).
14. **Pray for a spirit of Compassion.** "Love in action" (Mark 8:1-2).
15. **Pray for a spirit of Tenderness.** "A willingness to weep" (2 Kings 22:19).
16. **Pray for a spirit of Maturity.** "The capacity to grow" (Hebrews 5:12-14).
17. **Pray for a spirit of Holiness.** "Christ-like behavior" (1 Peter 1:16).
18. **Pray for a spirit of Reliability.** "A depth of dependability" (1 Corinthians 4:2).
19. **Pray for a spirit of Revelation.** "Learning to listen" (Ephesians 1:15,18).
20. **Pray for a spirit of Denial.** "A sacrifice to surrender" (Luke 9:23).
21. **Pray for a spirit of Confidence.** "The strength of the Lord" (Philippians 4:13).
22. **Pray for a spirit of Integrity.** "The quality of truthfulness" (Romans 12:17).
23. **Pray for a spirit of Repentance.** "A willingness to change" (Luke 3:8).

24. **Pray for a spirit of Trust.** "A fearless reliance" (Psalm 125:1).
25. **Pray for a spirit of Submission.** "Choosing to yield" (Ephesians 5:21).
26. **Pray for a spirit of Teachability.** "A quality of meekness" (Titus 3:2).
27. **Pray for a spirit of Prayer.** "A longing to wait" (Isaiah 40:31).
28. **Pray for a spirit of Unity.** "A respect for others" (1 Corinthians 1:10).
29. **Pray for a spirit of Restoration.** "A ministry of healing" (Isaiah 61:1-2).
30. **Pray for a spirit of Authority.** "A capacity to command" (Matthew 16:19).
31. **Pray for a spirit of Generosity.** "The desire to give" (Matthew 10:8).[2]

30 Ways to Pray for People in Authority

By Gary Bergel, President of Intercessors for America, www.ifapray.org

(Note: I have included this because I believe praying for those in authority is one of the most neglected responsibilities we have as praying people—youth or otherwise.)

The life of every citizen of every nation is affected by a vast multitude of individuals who wield significant influence each day. Consider: millions of elected officials, appointed judges, lawyers, police officers, bureaucrats, military officers, business executives and managers, those involved in church leadership, educators, medical practitioners and hospital administrators. How might we pray for these individuals? Here are thirty things based on scripture that we can pray for people in authority. Don't overwhelm yourself. Select one person or group of people and then pray one of these things each day for them.

1. That they be God fearing and recognize that they are accountable to Him for each decision and act (Proverbs 9:10).
2. That they be granted wisdom, knowledge, and understanding (James 1:5).
3. That they be presented with the gospel and loving Christian witness (Romans 10:14).
4. That they be drawn, if unsaved, to a saving encounter with Christ; if born-again, that they be strengthened and encouraged in their faith (1 Timothy 2:4; Ephesians 1:17-23).
5. That they recognize their own inadequacy and pray and seek the will of God (Proverbs 3:5-8; Luke 11:9-13).
6. That they be convicted of sin, transgression, and iniquity (Psalm 51:17; John 8:9).
7. That they heed their consciences, confess their sins, and repent (Proverbs 28:13; James 4:8).
8. That they read the Bible and attend prayer meetings and Bible studies (Psalm 119:11; Colossians 3:2).
9. That they value and regard the Ten Commandments and the teachings of Christ (Psalm 19:7-11; John 8:31-32).
10. That they respect and honor their own parents if living (Ephesians 6:2-3).
11. That they respect authority and practice accountability (Romans 13:1-7).

12. That they be given godly counsel and God-fearing advisors (Proverbs 24:6).

13. That they be honest and faithful to spouses and children (Malachi 2:15-16).

14. That they be practicing members of local congregations (Hebrews 10:25).

15. That they desire purity and avoid debauchery, pornography, perversion, and drunkenness (1 Corinthians 6:9-20; Titus 2:12).

16. That they be timely, reliable, and dependable (Matthew 21:28-31).

17. That they be honest in financial, tax, and ethical matters (1 Corinthians 6:10; 1 Timothy 6:6-10).

18. That they seek pastoral care and counsel when needed (Hebrews 13:7).

19. That they seek out and nurture godly friendships (Psalm 1:1-3).

20. That they have thankful and teachable spirits (Romans 1:21).

21. That they be generous and have compassionate hearts for the poor and needy (Psalm 112:9; Luke 10:33-37).

22. That they redeem their time and know priorities (Ephesians 5:15-17).

23. That they desire honesty, integrity, and loyalty (Psalm 26; Proverbs 11:3).

24. That they have courage to resist manipulation, bribery, pressure, and the fear of man (Proverbs 29:25; 2 Timothy 1:7).

25. That they be shielded from occultism, New Age cults, false religions, and secret societies (Isaiah 1:29, 2:6).

26. That they be presented with biblical worldviews and principles (Ephesians 3:10).

27. That they endeavor to restore the sanctity of life, families, divine order, and morality in our nation (Ephesians 5:22–6:1).

28. That they would work to reverse the trends of humanism, socialism, and statism in our nation (1 Chronicles 12:32; Isaiah 59:19).

29. That they desire humility and meekness and be willing to serve and cooperate (John 13:14; Titus 3:1-2).

30. That they be prepared to give account to Almighty God (Hebrews 9:27).[3]

Additional United Prayer Guidelines
By Eddie Smith, Cofounder and President of the U.S. Prayer Center, www.usprayercenter.org

Guidelines for Leaders
1. Be Spirit-led in order to lead in the Spirit.
2. Pray for wisdom ahead of time.
3. Prepare the room.
4. Review the guidelines with the group.
5. Discuss how you will find the Spirit's assignment.
6. Be spiritually discerning.
7. Be willing to confront and correct manipulators and monopolizers when necessary— earning the right to do so by loving others always and graciously understanding the difference between impurity and immaturity.
8. Remember that corporate unity is a higher goal in this situation than individual liberty.
9. Affirm and encourage.
10. Finish each prayer time with an instructional debriefing.

Guidelines for Participants
1. Come prepared to pray by stirring up your faith.
2. Sit together.
3. Speak up! Others cannot agree with what they cannot hear.
4. Avoid "preachy" praying and ministerial tones. Pray simply and conversationally.
5. Keep prayers concise, clear, and to the point.
6. Don't read long passages of Scripture.
7. Don't pray as you would in your private devotionals or pray through your personal prayer list.

8. Ask God, don't explain things to Him.
9. Avoid addressing others in the room under the pretense of prayer.
10. Once you have prayed, wait for other people to pray before praying again.
11. When in doubt about what to pray, ask for an outpouring of the Spirit on your church and city. All other requests are fulfilled when that occurs.
12. Try not to pray too big or too small. Pray for things the group can "get its faith around."
13. Don't be afraid of silence. It's sometimes golden.
14. Listen to, agree with, and affirm each pray-er.
15. Submit to pastor guidance.[4]

24-7 Movement Values

1. **Obedient to the Holy Spirit.** Like Jesus, we only seek to do what we see the Father doing. We acknowledge His right to break our rules and offend our sensibilities (John 5:19; Psalm 127:1; John 3:8).

2. **Relational.** We are a community of friends with shared vision and values, driven by friendship rather than function (John 15:14-15; Luke 10:1-22; 1 Peter 4:7-11; 1 John 4:7-12).

3. **Indigenous.** We respect, value, and honor cultural diversity (Revelation 7:9-10; Daniel 1; 1 Corinthians 9:20-21).

4. **Inclusive.** We work with anyone provided they share our vision and values, regardless of race, age, gender, or church background. We build unity and enjoy diversity (Colossians 3:11; Ephesians 4:3-6).

5. **Like Jesus.** We seek to be like Jesus in the way we do what we do. For us, the means do not necessarily justify the ends.

6. **Deeply Rooted.** We are committed to growth in maturity rather than size (Psalm 1:1-3).

7. **Creative and Innovative.** We embrace God-inspired creativity as integral to authentic expressions of prayer (Exodus 35:30-35; Genesis 1:1-2; Psalm 45:1; Proverbs 8:22-31).

8. **Just.** We will pursue justice and freedom from oppression for humanity and the created world (Isaiah 61; Luke 4:18-19; Romans 8:19-21; Isaiah 58).

9. **Good Stewards.** We take responsibility for ourselves, for those around us, and for the resources that God has entrusted to our care (Matthew 25:14-30; 2 Corinthians 9:6-15).

10. **Sacrificial.** We believe that a lifestyle of prayer is costly at every level (2 Corinthians 8:1-5; 1 John 3:16-18; Romans 12:1-2).

11. **Celebratory.** We believe that Jesus came to bring life to the full and that we have a Christian duty to celebrate all that is good. Fun and laughter are central to 24-7, and we do not need to justify these (Genesis 1:31; Psalm 24:1; Matthew 11:19; John 10:10).

12. **Simple.** We are a network of like-minded people, not some new slick organization. In character we are wild and unpolished, passionate about developing people rather than our own profile (Psalm 116:6; Luke 10:3-5; John 3:8).[5]

Higgs's Personal Recommendations: Books on/of/about Prayer

The Bible (surprise!)

á Kempis, Thomas, *The Imitation of Christ*

Benson, Robert, *Living Prayer*

Bounds, E. M., almost anything by this author

Brother Lawrence, *The Practice of the Presence of God*

Duewel, Wesley, *Mighty Prevailing Prayer*

Eastman, Dick, "Delight Trilogy": *Heights of Delight, Pathways of Delight,* and *Rivers of Delight*

Foster, Richard, *Prayer: Finding the Heart's True Home*

Murray, Andrew, almost anything by this author

Sheets, Dutch, *Intercessory Prayer*

Simpson, A. B., *The Life of Prayer*

Specific to Youth Ministry:

Baker, Jenny, *Transforming Prayers: 40 Unique Experiences for Youth Ministry*

Case, Steven L., *The Book of Uncommon Prayer*

Fuller, Cheri, *When Teens Pray*

Greig, Peter and Dave Roberts, *Red Moon Rising*

Jones, Tony, *Soul Shaper*

Notes

1. Source: "31 Biblical Prayers for Youth" by Dick Eastman. Used by permission.
2. Source: http://retirementwithapurpose.com/prayerforyouth.html
3. Source: *Pray!* magazine, www.navpress.com/Magazines/Pray! "30 Ways to Pray for People in Authority" by Gary Bergel. Used with permission.
4. Taken from the article by Eddie Smith, "Making It Work: How to Help Your Group Pray in One Accord," *Pray!* (Jan/Feb 1999), pp. 22-23. Reprinted with permission. See also the U.S. Prayer Center website, www.usprayercenter.org
5. Peter Greig and Dave Roberts, *Red Moon Rising* (Lake Mary, Fla.: Relevant Books, 2003), pp. 254-255.

Here's a resource to help you pray with more

Power, Passion, & Purpose

Every issue of *Pray!* includes:

- Powerful teaching by seasoned intercessors and prayer leaders
- Encouragement to help you grow in your prayer life—no matter at what level you are currently
- Exciting news stories on the prayer movement and prayer events around the world
- Profiles on people, organizations, and churches with unique prayer ministries
- Practical ideas to help you become a more effective prayer
- Inspirational columns to stimulate you to more passionate worship of Christ
- Classic writings by powerful intercessors of the past
- And much, much more!

Six issues of *Pray!* are only $19.97*

(*Plus sales tax where applicable. Canadian and international subscriptions are $25.97.)

Call **1-800-691-PRAY** (or 1-515-242-0297)
and mention code H4PRBKYMK when you place your order.

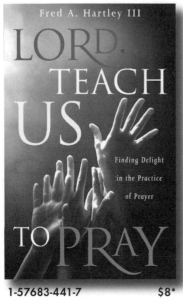

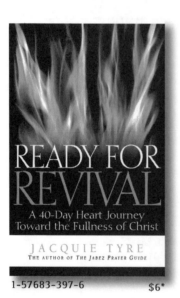